THE CONTENDERS

THE CONTENDERS

LAURA FLANDERS
RICHARD GOLDSTEIN
DEAN KUIPERS
JAMES RIDGEWAY
ELI SANDERS
DAN SAVAGE

SEVEN STORIES PRESS
New York ★ Toronto ★ London ★ Melbourne

Seven Stories Press
140 Watts Street
New York, NY 10013
www.sevenstories.com

In Canada: Publishers Group Canada, 559 College Street, Suite 402, Toronto,
ON M6G 1A9

In the UK: Turnaround Publisher Services Ltd., Unit 3, Olympia Trading
Estate, Coburg Road, Wood Green, London N22 6TZ

In Australia: Palgrave Macmillan, 15–19 Claremont Street, South Yarra VIC 3141

College professors may order examination copies of Seven Stories Press titles
for a free six-month trial period. To order, visit www.sevenstories.com/text-
book or send a fax on school letterhead to (212) 226-1411.

Book design by Jon Gilbert

Library of Congress Cataloging-in-Publication Data

The contenders : Hillary, John, Al, Dennis, Barack, et al. / Laura Flanders ...
[et al]. -- 1st ed.
    p. cm.
   ISBN 978-1-58322-789-3 (hardcover)
   1. Presidential candidates--United States--Biography. 2. Legislators--United
States--Biography. 3. Politicians--United States--Biography. 4. Democratic
Party (U.S.)--Biography. 5. Presidents--United States--Election--2008. 6.
United States--Politics and government--2001- I. Flanders, Laura.
E901.C66 5008
324.70973--DC22

                              2007036002

Printed in the USA.

9 8 7 6 5 4 3 2 1

Contents

Preface

AMY SCHOLDER

The build-up to the 2008 presidential election has been unprecedented. Never before has there been such a diversity of viable candidates (a woman, an African American, an Hispanic, an Alaskan, even a vegan). Never before has there been someone who is *not* running who has had such a direct impact on the political discourse. Never before has so much been inked and broadcast about these candidates, so early on in the pre-election game. And certainly, and most significantly, never before have the candidates raised and spent so much money to sustain their viability, and to spin their own images as much as possible.

But all this information—conveyed through print media, talk radio, the Internet, televised debates, memoirs, and exposés—has served to clog rather than clarify the situation. At times it seems like the frontrunners are interchangeable; at other times, it seems like a foregone conclusion that he/she who raises the most money wins. Because the political and electoral systems in this country have become so muddled, most of us are suspect of *anyone* who wants to run for president. And that leaves us with the perennial questions: who can I trust, and who will I vote for?

We asked six provocative and unflinching writers to focus attention on the Democratic Party contenders with the mandate to tell us something we don't know, but should, about each contender. They have done just that,

7

and in the process they have taught us about ourselves, as American citizens and as a culture. And they have made intriguing insights into the system within which these campaigns are designed and carried out. There is no better guide to the election, I believe, than one that doesn't tell you how to think or who to vote for, but instead tells you how each contender got to this stage, what they really stand for. The rest is up to you.

Clinton: Class of '68

LAURA FLANDERS

Hillary Clinton would not be as well-positioned to save the Democratic Party from its base if women in the United States had fewer reasons to be infuriated. As it is, the junior senator from New York just may be the party leaders' last best chance for rescue from angry and disgruntled Democratic voters.

At a time when the anti-war, anti-free trade Democrats are crying out for substantive change in their party and in the country, Clinton is able to cast herself as an agent of that change, even as her record and her policies promise, above all, cautious continuity. It's a feat made possible by the single fact that Clinton stands to be the first woman elected US president. In a less sexist world, it'd be hard for Clinton to present herself as any sort of political insurgent. Her husband is the country's favorite living president, and her campaign coffers are bulging with establishment dollars. In a sane world, this two-term senator from New York would be the ultimate insider. The US media, however, can always be relied upon to single out a woman for "outsider" treatment, and Hillary Clinton is no exception.

In the first week of June, 2007, the *New York Times* featured lengthy reviews of two unauthorized biographies: *Her Way: The Hopes and Ambitions of Hillary Rodham Clinton*, by Jeff Gerth and Don Van Natta, and *A Woman in Charge: The Life of Hillary Rodham Clinton*, by Carl

Bernstein. Gerth and Van Natta made the cover of the *Sunday Times Magazine* with an excerpt called "Hillary's War," while Bernstein droned on about Clinton's "ruthless ambition" and her "thick ankles" on public radio and TV. Meanwhile Bay Buchanan, the author of a third book, *The Extreme Makeover of Hillary (Rodham) Clinton*, gave interviews about Clinton's secretly radical feminist agenda on right-wing radio stations.

Against that media backdrop, the Hillary Clinton campaign held two big pep rallies. The first, a fundraising breakfast, hosted by "Women for Hillary" at the New York Hilton, attracted almost the full roster of New York City's female Congressional delegation. There were no cloth-covered tables, no flowers in vases, not even breakfast (only a snack in a paper sack)—but every straight-backed chair was occupied, and every face was trained on the stage. When feminist icon Billie Jean King (co-chair of "Women for Hillary") walked out on stage, every woman of a certain age in the audience remembered the day in 1973 when she beat the pants off of bigmouth Bobby Riggs in a game of champion tennis. King knows a thing or two about fighting back and winning. "Hillary's a fighter!" she said. "Hillary's a winner!" The crowd erupted. "This is the century for women," said King before introducing Clinton as "our champion, my friend, the next president . . ."

To cheers, Clinton finally strode on stage and high-fived King. "Am I ambitious? I don't mind the question, as long as every man in the race is asked the very same question," she said to more cheers.

Clinton will be the next president of the United States if crowds like this have anything to do with it. But it's not about love. Most of the women in the Hilton room that morning had plenty of qualms about Clinton's record, her husband's history, and about getting involved in another draining presidential race. Yet after scores of interviews, it's clear that the more that men, the media, and the Right beat up on the woman they call simply "Hillary," the more these women, even the progressives in the mix, will suppress their doubts and go to bat for her.

A middle-aged hospital worker volunteered at the Hilton convention before her shift. Although she personally supports single-payer national healthcare, rather than Hillary Clinton's private-insurer based plan, she believes Clinton deserves a second chance to reform the system: "Maybe this time she'll get it right," she whispered. "If they let her."

Martha Baker, a long-time advocate for women on welfare and women in nontraditional trades, strongly criticized Bill Clinton's signing of the 1996 welfare reform law ("but you can't blame Hillary for that," she says). She and her friend, author Letty Cottin Pogrebin (also at the Hilton that morning), wish Hillary would stop calling abortion "tragic." "It wasn't tragic for me," Pogrebin said brightly. "All that sort of talk sets us back." But both are adamant that Hillary Clinton is the Democrats' best candidate. "It's only sexism to have any doubt about that," Pogrebin asserts.

Former District Attorney Elizabeth Holtzman, who as congresswoman sat on the House committee investigating Richard Nixon, has just finished a book on the impeachable crimes of the Bush administration. Asked what she thought of Clinton's alleged failure to read in full the National Intelligence Council estimate on the Bush administration's claims about Saddam Hussein's possession of weapons of mass destruction before voting to give President Bush the authority to decide to declare war, Holtzman replied, "I'm disappointed. I disagreed with her vote on Iraq." But Holtzman is still backing the senator for president. "Ideologically, she's a cautious person, but I don't necessarily fault her for that." Added Holtzman, "I think it will be a great thing to have a woman president. Once that barrier's broken, it's broken forever."

Clinton's timing is perfect. After six disastrous years of the Bush presidency, the country as a whole is ready for change, and women like those Clinton's campaign is reaching out to believe change doesn't come bigger than the first woman in the White House—even if that woman has already spent eight years there married to a president.

Two days after the Hilton event, Club 44, a young women's campaign to elect Clinton as the forty-fourth president, kicked off with a $20 per ticket, open-air "block party" in Washington. Geraldine Ferraro, the only woman to represent a major US political party on a presidential ticket, took the stage and told the crowd, "Hillary is the candidate I've been waiting twenty-five years for."

Ferraro's not alone. Women of Hillary Clinton's generation have been waiting far longer than they ever expected for female leadership—in fact, for any kind of leadership that doesn't take them entirely for granted. Dolores Huerta, the grand dame of the United Farm Workers of America, served as Chair of "Women for Kerry" in 2004. She was appointed very late in the race, after urging from Los Angeles mayor Antonio Villaraigosa. Kerry gave Huerta no budget and virtually no staff; she says she was told not to talk about abortion or gay marriage, and she had to pay her own way to the party convention. Kerry once famously told a gathering of "Women for Kerry" that he wasn't going to single women out for attention, because he didn't want to "pander to a special interest." Never mind that women are the Democrats' single biggest voting block. Now the indomitable, white-haired Huerta is backing Hillary Clinton for president. She stood with Ferraro, King, and national campaign co-chair Ellen Malcolm, founder of the pro-choice fundraising group Emily's List, in the steamy summer sun on the Club 44 stage in Washington. Asked what lesson she'd bring from 2004 to 2008, Huerta didn't miss a beat: "The lesson from that campaign is *have a campaign.*"

It's a message Ann Lewis, Clinton's senior advisor, is taking to heart; that and the consistent lead that Clinton has maintained over her closest rivals thanks to the women's vote. In a June 2007 *Washington Post*-ABC News poll, Clinton led Senator Barack Obama of Illinois by a 2 to 1 margin among female voters. As the pollsters reported: "Her 15-point lead in the poll is entirely attributable to that margin." Clinton is drawing especially strong support from lower-income, lesser-educated women—voters Ann Lewis described to me as "women with needs." According to the *Washington Post*, in 2004, women made up a majority of the Democratic primary electorate, including between 54 and 59 percent in the early-voting states of New Hampshire, Iowa, and South Carolina.

Over 60 percent of the audience at Clinton's events is female, says Ann Lewis. The majority of these women, she says, come from outside of traditional political groups. Nurses, teachers, mothers—it is *their* networks the campaign plans to tap. "We're counting on networks of women—parents' associations, book clubs, sewing circles, you name it," Lewis told me. "This is the first campaign where we women have been out front from the beginning. I don't think you've ever seen a campaign that put women first."

Pat Reuss, senior policy analyst for NOW (the National Organization for Women), speaking in a private capacity, says she's ready to have a president in the White House who doesn't actively have it in for women and girls. "Hillary's a politician. She'll be a politician. But at least when she wakes up in the morning, somewhere in the top ten items on her to-do list will be something I care about. Mostly women aren't even on the list. Recently, we've been on the to-do-*against* list." As an activist who has spent much of the last thirty years lobbying Capitol Hill not to cut off federal funds to pay for poor women's abortions, and not to gag women's health professionals conducting federally funded family planning programs abroad, you can see what Reuss means. She lost both of those bitter fights. Then she watched right-wing lawyers eviscerate the enforcement provisions of the historic Violence Against Women Act for which she worked out her heart. The last twenty-five years have seen women's rights rolled back from the employment line to the pharmaceutical counter, where the latest fight is to protect a woman's right to fill a prescription for legal birth control. Censorious abstinence-only, sex mis-education projects run by conservatives have raked in $1 billion in federal tax dollars, while spending on just about everything else to do with sex and health has shrunk. States have passed parental consent laws by the score, and abortion clinics, along with the men and women who work there, are now under every possible constraint, including violence. In the US alone, seven people have been killed since 1990, including three doctors, two clinic employees, a security guard, and a clinic escort. The same administration that has unleashed an all out war on imagined threats abroad has done next to nothing to stop that form of terrorism.

For these reasons and more, it's not only so-called "second wave" women (of the 1970s movement) who say they are hoping for Hillary. In fact, the crowd at the Club 44 block party was equal parts over and under forty. Crystal Lander, the campus program director at the Feminist Majority Foundation (FMF), brought a dozen of her friends to the event. Independently, Lander volunteers with the Hillary Clinton campaign in Washington. By the time of the block party, she says, she'd already received invitations to fifteen different Clinton-related events. She's probably volunteered at the Clinton office ten times already. When the campaign announced a Women of Color luncheon with the senator, her email box filled up in less than two days with invitations from ten different, unconnected friends, many from her smart, black women's sorority, Alpha Kappa Alpha. "I don't remember anything like this level of excitement, this level of engagement, this early, since I was in Houston before George Bush was elected president," says Lander.

The comparison to Bush deserves a longer look. The second Bush and the second Clinton have more in common than family dynasties. As Bush did when he was a presidential candidate, Clinton casts herself as an agent of both change and continuity. Each has a former president in the family dragging his own baggage, and each talks up the "new," yet each draws on advisors that have familiar faces. (In Bush's case they were Dick Cheney and Donald Rumsfeld; in Clinton's, they are longtime family associates like Howard Ickes and former Democratic National Committee Chair Terry McAuliffe.) Perhaps most importantly, both George W. Bush and Hillary Clinton have grappled with a personal/political paradox. Clinton needs her party's activist base in 2008, like George W. did in 2000, yet the activists she needs to work on her behalf are exactly those who trust her least. To compound the problem, just as George W. did in 2000, Hillary Clinton seeks to replace an administration whose weaknesses lie exactly in the areas where she herself is weak.

Bush's bugaboos were the militarists and the Christian Right. The militarists didn't trust George's father, whose troops never entered Baghdad and whose moves to control the post-Cold War world they saw as slow and hesitant. George W.'s military record was nonexistent. The Christian Right too, was skeptical. The troublesome mob lying on Clinton's road to the White House is comprised of the fair trade populists and the anti-war movement.

In 2006, Democrats won their margins of victory in the Senate and the House thanks mostly to critics of the Iraq invasion and occupation and corporate globalized trade. Every single newly elected democratic senator is a critic of free-trade orthodoxy. The same is true of twenty-seven of twenty-nine Democratic pick-ups in the House. But the Clintons are champions of the globalized economy. Upon coming into office in 1992, Bill worked all-out to pass the

North American Free Trade Agreement, even against the complaints of the Democrats' friends in the environmentalist and labor movement. It was on his watch that labor unionists and Greens fought rain and angry Seattle cops to protest the World Trade Organization and its regime of big-is-best, race-to-the-bottom economics. Now courting labor and the environmentalist crowd, Hillary Clinton has come out against a trade pact with South Korea, but as senator, she has voted in support of free trade pacts with Oman, Chile and Singapore, even though she criticized them for what she said was their weak enforcement of international labor standards. In fact, she's voted for every trade agreement that has come before her except CAFTA, the Central American version of NAFTA, the pact the public has heard the most about.

The anti-war vote poses challenges to Clinton that are even more complex. Not only did her husband's administration maintain a cruel regime of sanctions and continuous bombing against Iraq throughout its eight years in office, but Hillary's own record in the senate makes her look more like Bush than anti-Bush.

The younger Bush, running on a campaign promise to restore "civility" to the White House after Bill Clinton, faced a problem: as a known drinker and carouser, he had to reinvent himself. He pulled it off. From the draft-dodging ugly duckling emerged the sober puffed-up patriarch, cocksure in fighter-pilot suit. The man Texas wit Molly Ivins teased converted himself from Shrub to Christian crusader to continuing, deadly, effect. Hillary Clinton has a more delicate reinvention ahead, because it's not just her behavior, it's her biology that is considered problematic for anyone running to be commander in chief.

Clinton has taken the Margaret Thatcher approach to the problem of being female. From her first days running for office, she's presented herself as America's version of Britain's first female Prime Minister, a woman who once said "There is no such thing as society. There are individual men and women, and there are families." As soon as she entered the Senate, Clinton's image-makers emphasized security, defense, and personal strength. Comparing Clinton to Thatcher, McAuliffe told the *Sunday Times* of London, "Their policies are very different but they are both perceived as very tough."[1]

Within hours of two planes crashing into two New York towers on September 11, 2001, Hillary Clinton's closest advisor, Bill, urged her to come out strong. According to a Clinton advisor interviewed by biographers Van Natta and Gerth, it was he who encouraged her to show that she had the requisite boldness and guts to lead the nation and protect her people. The very next day, Hillary delivered a call to arms that hailed "wrath" on those who harbored terrorists. While others, notably Mary Robinson (the former president of Ireland and at the time, the sitting United Nations High Commissioner for Human Rights), were modeling a different style of leadership by holding firm for global cooperation, criminal prosecution, and a reassertion, rather than a shredding of international jurisprudence, Clinton channeled Thatcher, Britain's "Iron Lady," and delivered a bombastic speech in which she described the attacks on the World Trade Center and Pentagon as an "attack on America." Clinton called for punishment for those responsible, the hijackers, and their ilk and vowed that any country that chose to harbor terrorists and "in any way aid or comfort them whatsoever will now face the wrath of our country." Bush apparently liked what he heard. He echoed her language and issued an almost identical threat, eight days later, in his address to Congress.

Coming out of the gate for the use of force, Clinton put herself on a collision course with those like Mary Robinson who were calling the attacks of 9/11 criminal acts, not acts of war. She set in place a Bush/Clinton alliance that haunts Hillary as a presidential candidate every time she attempts to cast herself as his alternative. On the campaign trail, and especially in televised debates, Clinton is at pains to frame the so-called war on terror as "Bush's war," but she's had an active part in it. It isn't as if her 9/11 speech was an exception. Clinton supported Bush's invasion and bombardment of Afghanistan. She voted for the USA PATRIOT Act, which gave the government new unconstitutional tools of search and seizure even as federal agents were sweeping thousands of innocent civilians off the streets of US cities, notably in New York. When the US-led invasion of Iraq lay in the balance, pending a vote in Congress, Hillary rose in the Democrat-controlled Senate and voted to give the president the authority he sought to decide to attack. But Clinton not only gave Bush and Cheney her vote, she embraced their argument, saying that Iraqi president Saddam Hussein had "worked to rebuild his chemical and biological weapons stocks . . . and his nuclear program." Alone among Democratic Senators, she accused Iraq's leader of giving "aid, comfort and sanctuary to terrorists, including Al Qaeda members." That link, so shamelessly pushed by the Bush administration, was always doubted by most in so-called "intelligence"—and most Democrats, not to mention war critics. It was later publicly debunked as false.

In her autobiography, *Living History*, she describes her vote on October 10, 2002, as "probably the hardest decision I have ever had to make." In televised debates and in her autobiography she insists she believed she was voting for more diplomacy, not for "any new doctrine of preemption, or for unilateralism." Yet had she truly wanted to require more diplomacy and put some brakes on Bush, she could have done it. Carl Levin and several other Senate Democrats introduced an amendment that required the UN pass a new resolution explicitly approving the use of force against Iraq. It also required the president to return to Congress if his UN efforts failed. Clinton remained silent as eleven other senators debated it for ninety-five minutes and ultimately joined the majority of seventy-five senators who voted against.

Six years later, a majority of the country, including 90 percent of Clinton's Democratic base, not only thinks the war was wrong, they want the troops out of Iraq.[2] Clinton is still prevaricating on the troop deployment. "That's what I'm working on, to get them out," she told hecklers from the women's peace group, CodePink, at a liberal activists' gathering in DC in June, 2007. But even as she spoke, her official policy was for a "phased redeployment," which still involves tens of thousands of US troops stationed indefinitely in and around Iraq. She shares the Bush/Cheney view of who is to blame—and it's not those who approved the deployment, and certainly not the conduct of the US troops. "The American military has succeeded. It's the Iraqi government which has failed," continued Clinton in her speech in DC, to which not only Code Pink but almost the entire crowd booed.

Can Clinton successfully reinvent this part of herself? It's not just her candidacy that's in the balance; it's Bill's legacy, part of which is wrapped up in Iraq. The Clinton administration supported a brutal sanctions regime and regular bombing of Iraq on the grounds that Saddam Hussein was developing nuclear and chemical weapons. In many ways, Clinton's doctrine of "humanitarian intervention" in Somalia and Yugoslavia (but not Rwanda), laid the intellectual groundwork for Bush's rhetoric of "preemptive attack," in that both rest on the notion that the US has a *special* role in the world (and can therefore exempt itself from international rules of conduct that other nations must not break).

There's a political legacy in the balance too—the whole big-dollar, big-influence style of campaigning and governance that both Clintons have finessed. Since she entered the senate in 2001, no senator has raised more money than Clinton has—$51.5 million, according to the Center for Responsive Politics. Her personal political action committee, HILL-PAC, is one of the biggest money-raisers and spenders in the business. For her 2008 presidential bid, she set a goal of $100 million raised through the primaries. To reach her target, she's decided to forgo public financing, just as Bush did in 2000 and 2004. While Barack Obama has decided to reject donations from political action committees and lobbyists, Hillary has embraced the politics of the Penthouse Party. Raising money in the suites, she hopes to send her campaign workers out to flood the streets, and in most primary states to date she's doing just that. In early June 2007, the Clinton campaign had more paid workers in New Hampshire (fifty-four) than every other Democrat combined.[3]

☆　☆　☆

Clinton is in a money race with Obama, but she's in another race too: some call it the quest for "magic." Obama, as a state senator, didn't need access to high level "intelligence" to oppose the Iraq War. He spoke out against it for all the right reasons before it started, and he was an early adopter of the rhetoric "troops out." (Like Clinton's, his concrete plan, however, sounds less like "out" than "partly out.") Obama's charisma and his best-selling books attract him huge crowds—20,000 in Austin, Texas in February, for example, when the Democratic primaries were still a year off. His record as a state senator, especially on civil liberties, is strong. Obama sponsored successful legislation to combat racial profiling and to protect police detainees during interrogation. He sponsored an unsuccessful bill banning discrimination against lesbians and gays. His talk of faith and the goodness of America's "heart," moves hearts, especially young hearts, and he's built up a base of small dollar donors that's matching, even outpacing, Clinton's cash-box.

North Carolina's John Edwards has a reputation for working hard. Although he's a multi-millionaire like the rest of the candidates, he's rarely seen in a shirt that doesn't have its sleeves rolled up. He draws on his father's history as an Appalachian mill-worker. ("If I hear that story one more time I'll scream," one Nevada union organizer told me.) Unlike Hillary Clinton, he not only speaks eloquently of the "Two Americas"—rich and poor—he has actually broken with the pro-corporate Democratic Leadership Council, which pretty much created Clintonomics. While Clinton was confronting her record, which includes six years of service on the board of directors of Wal-Mart (1986-92), Edwards was out the street in Pittsburgh rallying with an anti-Wal-Mart group. In a break with the rest of the 2008 Democratic pack (except Dennis Kucinich), he has declared that reducing the deficit—the most bally-hooed accomplishment of the Clinton Administration—is less important to him than spending government money on what people need, like healthcare and reconstruction on the Gulf Coast. He has called for an end to poverty in the US over the next thirty years by spending $15 billion each year—it sounds more like LBJ than Hillary Rodham. Finally, he has broken from the conventional consultant pack. Clinton's chief strategist, Mark Penn (a key operative from Bill Clinton's 1996 race), runs a public relations firm that specializes in spin for union busters, Shell Oil, and big tobacco companies. Edwards's 2008 campaign is being run by David Bonior, a former Michigan congressman who strongly opposed NAFTA and welfare reform.

Only Dennis Kucinich proposes single-payer, nonprofit healthcare, publicly financed elections, and a department of peace.

If either Edwards or Obama—or for that matter any of Clinton's challengers—won the nomination, it would be a break in some significant respect from old school Democratic Party politics. At least in the framing, if not in much of the substance of his policy proposals, Obama is casting his campaign as an up-from-below, new v. old, youth v. elders contest. His nomination would be a strike against the good-old-white-boy network. Edwards is pledging a return to the rhetoric and maybe even the policies of the New Deal. A win by either candidate, not to mention the other contenders, could rightfully be claimed by anti-war, fair-trade voters as a victory against the Democratic Party establishment. The job Hillary has signed up for is to win her party's nomination—and then the country—while keeping the party status quo mostly in place. Clinton is seeking the nomination without a record of dissent from Bush on the use of force to solve problems abroad. She's also hoping that by muttering things about "reviewing" NAFTA she won't have actually to break with her husband's tainted policies on domestic spending and trade. Looking towards the general election, she's counting on winning the it the same old way, running a big-budget, cutthroat campaign, financed by all the usual suspects. Hillary's task is to dress her establishment-self up in just enough rebel's clothing to pacify the critics before the primary, and then win over enough alienated voters in November—probably by persuading them that she'll change some things, but not too many.

She just might manage it. While most of the media's reporting on Hillary is fixated on her relations with Bill, it's her individual experience that stands her in good stead for this moment. Years before she met Bill Clinton she was developing exactly the skills that her party's savior will need in 2008—the skills of an anti-agitator. In those, she's an expert.

The last time Democrats faced a serious anti-war insurgence was forty years ago, in 1968. Hillary, who'd grown up in a Republican household led by a draconian pro-GOP dad, campaigned for Barry Goldwater as a teenager, walking immigrants' blocks in downtown Chicago checking for "vote fraud" benefiting Democrats. In her freshman year in college she was elected president of Wellesley's College Republicans. That summer, the summer of 1968, she attended the Republican National Convention as guest of Republican congressman Melvin Laird of New York (she had just wrapped up an internship assigned to the House Republican Conference). In Miami, she watched the GOP nominate not the moderate she liked, Governor Nelson Rockefeller, but Richard Nixon. With dismay, she concluded that "the nomination of Richard Nixon cemented the ascendance of the conservative over the moderate" in Republican ranks.[4]

The scene on the Democratic front was disconcerting to Clinton too. A few weeks after Nixon's nomination, she watched the turmoil at the Democratic National Convention, which was held in Chicago in 1968. On summer break at her parents' house in suburban Park Ridge, Hillary drove with a friend into town to "observe" anti-war protestors clash with Chicago cops in Grant Park, while Democratic delegates over at the International Amphitheater fought over who to nominate: Senator Eugene McCarthy (D-MN), who advocated immediate withdrawal from Vietnam, or Hubert Humphrey, who favored a gradual draw-down contingent on concessions from the North Vietnamese.

If the GOP under Nixon lost its appeal for Hillary that year, she's very quiet about what she thought of the Democrats. (As she wrote, it wasn't she who quit the GOP: "I sometimes think that I didn't leave the Republican Party as much as it left me.") As a "heart liberal" and a "mind conservative" (as she once described herself in a letter to a friend), Clinton was seeking moderation in an immoderate era. She was certainly not swept up in the tumultuous passions of her age. Of all the nominees on offer that year, she chose the slow withdrawer. She was just twenty-one, and her registration didn't take effect in time to vote, but she later said she would have voted for Humphrey. When Nixon trounced Humphrey, it was only logical for her to wonder how a "moderate" (read, "centrist") could learn from a conservative the necessary tricks to win power and gain office.

"Outside-in" activism wasn't Hillary's way. Although she'd been introduced to Dr. Martin Luther King, Jr., by one of her high school mentors, Don Jones, and writes that she was inspired by the civil rights movement, grassroots community organizing wasn't her thing. The popular guru of "people power" organizing, Saul Alinsky, was a Chicago man. When he got the chance, Barack Obama, a fellow Chicagoite, went to work for an Alinsky-inspired group after graduating Columbia (before law school at Harvard). Seventeen years earlier, Hillary chose instead to write a college paper on a group inspired by Alinsky—the Community Action Program. After studying the group for weeks, she came away unimpressed. "[Alinsky] believed you could change the system only from the outside. I didn't," she wrote bluntly in *Living History*.

While Clinton was at Yale in 1970, she was faced with another inside/outside conflict. Bobby Seale and seven other Black Panther leaders went on trial for murder in downtown New Haven. The case focused attention on— and ignited anger at—the federal government's insidious

Counter-Intelligence Program (COINTELPRO). Twelve thousand Panther supporters flooded into the area, many housed by Clinton's classmates. She didn't describe her feelings about the protestors outside the courtroom in her coverage of Seale's trial for the campus paper. What she does report in her autobiography is that when an enormous May Day protest climaxed in an arson attack on a campus library building, she joined the staff and faculty's bucket brigade to douse the flames and manned an arson-alert team for the rest of the semester. You could say she's been a flame-douser ever since.

Hillary got a closer look at Nixon's way of doing things when, in 1974, she was invited to join the lawyers working for the House Judiciary Committee then considering his impeachment. (Actually, Bill was invited, but he declined, recommending his new squeeze, a fellow Yale-ite.) Hillary was tasked with drawing up an organizational map, laying out how Nixon's White House worked. It was strictly hierarchical, she concluded, but Nixon was all over it. His hands were in every detail, tracking every player's part. She also spent hours listening to Nixon's voice on subpoenaed tapes, and even to the voice of Nixon reviewing his own voice on what was called the "tape of tapes." The president would listen and try to justify what he'd said in order to deny or minimize his involvement in criminal acts. "It was extraordinary to listen to Nixon's rehearsal for his own cover-up," she wrote.

Clinton's speech patterns leave people in no doubt about her smarts, but they do leave some wondering if she is capable of speaking from the heart. At her rallies, Clinton has a careful, calculating way of speaking. It's as if she's thinking three times about every word. Perhaps she's playing tapes back in her head. One thing is clear: by the time "tricky Dick" was forced out of office, his investigator had absorbed a few tricks, even some that betray her. Clinton's preferred organizational structure is hierarchical. "Hillaryland," as her senior staff are known, are loyal—and obedient—to a fault. Her campaign's treatment of the press is harsh (even "Nixonian," as reporter David Brock called it in his Clinton biography). At Club 44, all the journalists were cooped up in a pen, and handlers strictly forbade reporters from mingling even with the friendly crowd. And like Nixon, Clinton is famous for having a finger in every pie. When the decision of the day was which theme song to choose for the 2008 race, the candidate is said to have spent two full hours on the conference call (only to choose the cheesy Canadian crooner, Celine Dion, over every US competitor, including the outspoken Dixie Chicks).

Nixon had a vision of a constituency, which he succeeded in building where Goldwater flopped. He built a new GOP majority out of disaffected, mostly white, post civil rights, southern Democrats. In a time of turmoil, he looked for the "invisible" voters, those who weren't in the streets. In a speech young Hillary most likely saw or later read at the convention in Miami Beach in 1968, Nixon appealed to the "forgotten Americans." His speechwriter on that occasion, Ray Price, later said, "that was something that was very important. The mobs were burning cities, they were rioting, the war in Vietnam was brutally unpopular. The counterculture was really making its thrust, tearing things apart. And he was trying to get beyond that . . . he was basically appealing over the heads of the rioters to the majority to take control of their country again, and take control of their lives, and put it back on track."[5] Soon thereafter, the "forgotten Americans" became Nixon's catchphrase: "The silent majority." Clinton talks about "invisible Americans" in her stump speeches. In a new time of turmoil, she is counting on them to create a majority, as Nixon's majority did, that will outweigh those who would "tear things apart."

"America's middle class and working families have become the invisible Americans," Clinton says. "If you are a hardworking single parent who can't afford health insurance, or a small business owner who worries about energy costs, or a student who can't afford to continue college, you are invisible to the oil companies earning record profits while you pay more at the pump. You are invisible to the companies who outsource your job or lay you off."

To Clinton in 2007, as to Nixon in 1968, the "invisible Americans" are preferable to the visible sort: the marching-in-the-street sort, who might mention the relationship between her husband's NAFTA and that outsourced job. The "invisible Americans" are certainly more appealing a constituency than those voters who made themselves visible in November 2006, and expected the new Democratic majority in Congress to show bold leadership on Iraq, on torture, on poverty, and trade.

Clinton's field organizing in the states, early on, has been stellar: monied, methodical, and smart. Her team makes a habit of plugging into grassroots groups like ACORN (whose support has been indispensable to her in New York)

as well as to what she calls "grass-tops"—community leaders and local legislators. In New Hampshire, as early as June 2007, a staff assistant for Congresswoman Carol Shea Porter described Clinton's campaign as "flawless," the only risk being that there's little room left for the kind of spontaneity that keeps volunteers excited. In Nevada, where the party's caucuses will be held very early in the campaign schedule in 2008, every candidate is lobbying hard for the kind of influential "grass-top" endorsements that have the power to turn party faithful out to caucus. Local politicos were surprised when one of the most powerful men in the state, Senate Leader Harry Reid's son Rory (who chairs Las Vegas's all powerful Clark County Gaming Commission) signed up early in 2007 to co-chair Clinton's campaign in the state. By mid-July 2007, it was hard to find a single Democratic legislator in Nevada, Iowa, or New Hampshire who hadn't received a call or a visit from the woman-who-would-be president. "She gets it," says Gail Tuzzolo, veteran political consultant for the influential Nevada AFL-CIO. Nevada state senator Dina Titus, a popular feminist and environmentalist who ran for governor in 2006, is heading up a campaign group called "Women of the West," which Ann Lewis says will have her stumping for women's votes all over the western states.

It could be a hidden advantage for Clinton that the labor movement is morphing from blue-collar to pink. The fastest growing sector of the workforce today is in service and female dominated jobs. In Nevada, the union that dominates the heavily populated south of the state is the casino, hotel, and restaurant worker's union known colloquially as "the Culinary." With plenty of staff time to spend on research, Clinton comes to every local event fully prepped.

In Las Vegas, when she met with the members of Culinary Local 226, she talked about her experience bussing tables. The members, who spend back-breaking days carrying heavy trays and fending off gropers, were impressed. "It really resonated," Pilar Weiss, political director for Local 226 told me. "Our members left here psyched."

Much as the typically male, DC-based campaign consultants may doubt it, it's those women who will actually wear holes into their shoes walking blocks to turn out the vote. The question is, in a long campaign, will the candidate's positions keep her supporters hooked in long enough, fervently enough, to keep them motivated? In several key early primary or caucus states, the political winds are favoring women. New Hampshire has the largest percentage of elected women in the country. The state sent its first woman to Congress in 2006 (Carol Shea Porter, who ran on an anti-war platform); the speaker of the New Hampshire House is a woman; and so is the president of the state senate. In Nevada too, the Speaker of the House is female for the first time; Barbara Buckley, who ran for governor, another first. At the state level, women have been making gains, but the energy of a local campaign doesn't necessarily transfer to a national candidate. As Scott Nichols, staff assistant to Shea Porter, put it, "any presidential campaign is going to be about insiders and insider issues. And that's the opposite of what stirs the grassroots."

While Edwards and Obama are each in their own way running as "outsiders" who promise relief from the status quo in Washington, Clinton's campaign is at pains to paint her as the most qualified and most experienced candidate in the race. The most often heard comment about

Clinton from her supporters is that she will be able to hit the ground running once she's elected president, because she knows how Washington works. But the qualities that she believes will persuade on-the-fence conservatives to trust her, namely her experience and her ability to get along in Washington, are exactly the qualities that turn off voters like those who turned out in 2006 to bring about real change in government. The most successful presidential candidates are different from Senators; they make certain issues central and campaign on them even against resistance (reforming welfare, say, in Bill Clinton's case, or cutting taxes, in George W. Bush's). Candidates who seek to be national leaders, as opposed to effective legislators, inspire people when they model leadership.

Hillary is a compromiser and always has been. She makes no bones about it. "I'm cursed with the responsibility gene," she's written.[6] That doesn't mean she can't stand and fight. She's done that on occasion, most notably to defend her husband. In 1992, when Gennifer Flowers emerged from Bill Clinton's past with a story to tell, Hillary made a back-channel contact to an old friend in San Francisco and hired a shark of a private eye to track down the rest of Bill's paramours. The investigator, Jack Palladino, was under instructions to wrest from the targeted women signed affidavits denying any sexual or romantic involvement. When he encountered resistance he'd interview family and lovers until he'd dug up just enough compromising material to persuade the women to zip their lips.

In 1999 Hillary Clinton was adamant about the bombing of Belgrade. While her husband's generals were in doubt about which tactics to use against the Serb nationalist Slobodan Milosevic (for fear that bombing, as opposed to deploying ground troops, would accelerate ethnic cleansing in Kosovo), Hillary reports that she stood firm: "I urged him to bomb," she told a reporter."[7] "You've got to bite the bullet," she told the president. (Bombing did indeed lead to an acceleration of Serb atrocities, but after eleven weeks of round the clock air strikes the Milosevic regime crashed.)

Politically she is no strategic slouch, but her strategy has always been to move towards bipartisanship and to the right. According to Sheehy, it was Hillary who persuaded Bill to take the chairmanship of the Democratic Leadership Council in 1990. The Council, which Bill Clinton had helped found, was seeking to redirect the party away from the Left. In return, the DLC gave him the resources to travel the country and try out his "New Democrat" agenda on the public. Although there were personal troubles in the Clintons' marriage, they were constant colleagues when it came to political work. In May 1991, Clinton delivered the keynote at a DLC convention, laying out the vision they'd hammered out together: "Opportunity, responsibililty, community." DLC activist Al Fromm was blown away, "People said it was the first time they'd heard a moderate Democrat speak with passion. They loved him."[8] Hillary's inner Nixon must have been proud.

Forced to choose between the Nixon way and the McCarthy way, Clinton will always choose the Humphrey way, and even her positions on what to others would be be bedrock issues waver and shift. When she arrived in Arkansas in 1974, she was an opponent of the death penalty. She changed her views sometime between her husband's service as attorney general and governor. By the time 1992 rolled around, she and Bill took time off from the Presidential campaign to return to Little Rock to preside over the execution of Ricky Ray Rector, a brain-damaged African American convicted of killing a police officer.

On a visit to Gaza City in 1998, she met with Palestinian Authority leader Yasir Arafat and his wife and declared, well ahead of the official line from the White House, her support for a Palestinian state. Her husband's spokesperson had to distance him from her comment. As a senator, however, one of her first major speeches was to AIPAC, the Israeli lobby group where she pledged to work to send more money, not for peacekeeping, or to both sides, but for Israel's military. (She's spoken to AIPAC many times since.) On the fortieth anniversary of the Israeli occupation of West Bank and Gaza, Clinton joined the rest of the Senate in sending a message of congratulation and support to the Israeli government. No encouraging message went to the Palestinians still enduring occupation.

Clinton talks up her commitment to women and children. One of her first jobs out of college was with Marion Wright Edelman, and later she co-chaired Edelman's Children's Defense Fund. Yet when the GOP proposed a draconian welfare law that eliminated entitlements and put poor mothers' assistance in the hands of the states, Clinton supported her husband signing the bill into law even as Edelman's husband and her good friend, Peter Edelman, warned that the cruel legislation would move some 2.6 million people, including 1.1 million children, into poverty. The law cut off almost 800,000 legal immigrants entirely, and denied them Supplemental Security Income (SSI) and food stamps. An assistant secretary for planning and evaluation at the Department of Health and Human Services, Edelman resigned in protest. "After all this noise and heat about balancing the budget, the only deep, multi-year budget cuts actually enacted [1994-96] were those in this bill, affecting low-income people," he wrote in the *Atlantic Monthly* shortly afterwards.[9]

Edelman says his old friend Hillary wrote him a note afterwards inviting a conversation, but he was never sure of her views about the bill. In *Living History* she says she encouraged her husband privately to soften the childcare and children's healthcare provisions in the law, but in the end she sums up the situation: "Welfare reform became a success for Bill."[10]

"It wasn't a success for us," recalls Delana Lewis, a student at the City University of New York. Research shows that 90 percent of people receiving assistance in 1996 were women with children. Eighty-eight percent of those who were able to attain a bachelor's degree moved to jobs with a living wage and out of poverty. In 1995, there were 27,000 students like Lewis, receiving public assistance while they studied at CUNY. Ten years later, after the law pushed recipients' workfare requirements up and limited exemptions for education, there were just 5,000. "For us it was disastrous," Lewis told me a few days after Hillary's Hilton Breakfast. "We lost over 20,000 students. Lines at the shelters became longer, finding quality childcare became a joke." Lyn Loeur, another Hunter student, witnessed the impact on her working parents, recent immigrants from Cambodia: "It changed everything. It killed poor people's hopes," she told me.

Peter Edelman wrote an entire book about his experiences. On welfare reform, he knew where all the major players in the administration at the time stood—except for one. "I knew were [Harold] Ickes stood. I knew George Stephanopolous's views. But I never knew Hillary's," Edelman told me. No topic was more central to their close friendship, one that went back more than twenty years, and yet her views remained invisible to her friend.

By her own account, Hillary took the quiet route on welfare reform: "although I stayed out of the public debate, I actively participated in the internal one. I made it clear to Bill and his policy advisers in the West Wing that if I thought they were caving into a mean-spirited Republican bill that was harmful to women and children, I would publicly oppose it." But after two vetoes, President Clinton eventually signed a mean-spirited bill, and if she opposed it, she didn't speak out.

While Hillary Clinton almost never mentions Nixon, she is famously fond of recalling former First Lady Eleanor Roosevelt. One wonders how Hillary's inner Nixon and her inner Eleanor mix. She once got in trouble with the media for saying she "talked" to Eleanor in her head. Roosevelt was certainly no stranger to kitchen table prodding and wifely persuasion, but she was a leader too, and she pushed her husband in public on critical issues including civil liberties, poverty, and segregation. She wrote dozens of columns, hosted a radio show, and held her own regular news conferences with the press. Roosevelt certainly took her hits from the media and the public, but she helped advance issues she cared about, including human rights. As Blanche Wiesen Cook, her biographer, reflects, "Human rights, torture, detention without trial; spying, disappearances, an out-of control executive. All the things we're dealing with now. That's what Eleanor spoke about. Where is Hillary?" There's something to be said, after all, for an intellectual arsonist.

Hillary Clinton has taken hits—for her early writings on children's legal rights, for her activism in women's issues (she compiled three editions of a *Handbook on Legal Rights for Arkansas Women*), and most spectacularly for the failure of her healthcare effort. Media misogynists hold nothing back: the attacks on the first lady have always been personal and vicious, and for years they wouldn't let up. Her looks, her parenting skills, her sexuality, even her daughters' teeth were deemed acceptable targets for right-wing talk radio and the press. To this date there are scores of Hillary Clinton websites, mostly negative. And she still takes hits from the media darlings of the Right. Media lollygagger and right wing loony, Ann Coulter got into trouble for joking about calling John Edwards a "faggot," but six months earlier, in her nationally syndicated column, Coulter wrote: "I'd say that's about even money" on Senator Clinton "[c]oming out of the closet" in 2008, and the public response was mostly silence.

The pillorying of Hillary can work to her advantage. As feminist *Nation* columnist Katha Pollitt put it, "If people keep making sexist attacks on Hillary Rodham Clinton, I may just have to vote for her."[11] But amid the barrage of media sexism, it's easy to lose focus on the substance of Clinton's policies. Look more closely and it's clear that when it comes to most contentious issues, Hillary has made a habit of dodging. As one critic, Donna Stanton, first female editor of the Modern Languages Assocation journal says, she wants it both ways: "She wants to be seen as smart and a leader, and she wants to dodge." Of Clinton's famous Iraq vote, giving president Bush the authority to decide to wage war, Stanton says, "she wants us to believe she's the smartest woman in the room and she was also misled. I wasn't misled. Lots of people weren't misled." Since Clinton entered the Senate, she has taken the lead on defending the so-called "morning after pill" as well as RU 486, and she has fought to increase the childcare provisions in the reauthorized welfare law. But there's a far longer list of leadership opportunities she has missed, from failing to sign on to Sen. Diane Feinstein's (D-CA) bill to ban the US from using or selling cluster bombs (like those used by the US in Iraq or in Lebanon by Israel) to ignoring Rep. Maxine's Waters's (D-CA) pleas for a senator to sponsor a version of her bill (passed in the House in March 2007) that would shore up oversight of reconstruction in the Gulf and protect public housing and public education in New Orleans.

Shortly after the 2004 election (which was spuriously said to have been decided on "moral issues"), Clinton co-authored an op-ed piece with Harry Reid (D-NV, an opponent of abortion rights), calling on pro-choicers to find "common ground" with abortion opponents. In a speech to the Family Planning Association of New York, she not only called (as her husband did) for abortion to be "safe, legal and rare," she called abortion a sad, "even tragic," choice, language that sells down the river any notion that a woman has a right to terminate a pregnancy to save her hopes and dreams (not to mention her existing kids or the elder parents she's caring for).

After the passage of the welfare law, Hillary Clinton writes that she realized she'd become a "politician, no longer policy advocate." Finding "common ground" as she has done with politicians Democrats despise—like

Newt Gingrich (who led the "angry white male" GOP revolt in 1994) is what Hillary sees as the way to get good things done, but it's no way to move political ground or fuel up a movement. Ellen Bravo, author of *Taking on the Big Boys: Why Feminism is Good for Families, Business and the Nation*, and for many years the head of the working women's organization 9 to 5, said that when Clinton tried to make her opinions on abortion more nuanced, she missed "a huge opportunity" to criticize the hypocrisy of those who claim to care about "life" but oppose measures to improve women's access to healthcare, birth control, and living wages. "She missed an opportunity to lead."

Promising to make political change, Hillary Clinton is seeking to fire up voters, especially women voters, with the promise that she'll change the climate in Washington and shift the political debate. But the debate and the laws that so many women care about have moved to the right, in no small part because of exactly the sort of conciliatory speech that Hillary Clinton is best at delivering. For example, the assault on legal abortion has come about because the flame-throwers of the Right were not hesitant to speak out. While liberal pro-choicers sought "common ground" with abortion's foes, the Right, with its radical agenda, changed not only laws but attitudes and vocabulary—including attitudes towards women, their doctors and their advocates—and they fired up mass movements.

The energy Hillary Clinton's campaign hopes to run on is movement energy: specifically, as on display at "Women for Hillary" events, women's movement energy spilling over from the 1970s. But half the people in the crowd at the Club 44 weren't even born when Billie Jean King thrashed tennis jock Riggs in straight sets. They certainly weren't born when Dolores Huerta led farm workers out of the fields and into the streets for their rights. The organized women's movement has never regained the passion and thrust it had in the 1970s. On the contrary, it has taken thirty years of hits, setting back its agenda, its power in Washington and its organizational strength. Across the country, as Clinton's campaign seeks to tap into women's networks, it is up against the reality that, in contrast to their opponents, women's rights groups have almost entirely avoided party politics. Planned Parenthood endorsed a presidential candidate for the very first time in 2004, but the four-million-strong group is not issuing any endorsement in the Democratic primary. Emily's List endorsed Hillary Clinton, but it was a first—they've never endorsed a primary candidate and have no experience in national primaries. (They failed to endorse Carole Moseley Braun when she ran for the nomination in 2004.) The Feminist Majority is a tax-exempt 501c3 organization, which is banned under the tax code from taking an active role in party politics. (The Majority's Eleanor Smeal is backing Clinton, but in a personal capacity.) The National Organization for Women's Political Action Committee (NOW-PAC) endorsed Hillary Clinton almost as soon as she entered the primary, and has chapters in all fifty states as well as state-based Political Action Committees that may contribute to state-level candidates. But national campaign finance law makes it very hard for any national PAC to put much money into federal elections.

"In federal races, there's very little we can do," NOW's national president Kim Gandy explained. NOW-PAC can contribute $5,000 to Clinton in the primary and $5,000 in the general, but that's it. "What we can do is email our members, encourage our people to volunteer and mobilize their book clubs, their synagogues, their gardening circles—and hold house parties."

NOW's former staff are well-embedded across the country. Harriet Trudell, for example, former State Director of NOW in Nevada, is now political Director of the State Democratic Party. That may add to her enthusiasm for Clinton in the General, but it won't help Clinton in the primary (the state party won't endorse any candidate). PPFA, now under the directorship of Cecile Richards, won't be endorsing a candidate in the 2008 primaries, says Richards, because "The Democrats have an embarrassment of riches in terms of primary candidates, and we want to work with any one of them." PPFA's supporters are unusually excited about the election, Richards continues: "They're excited about Clinton, but also Obama, and they love Elizabeth Edwards."

Assuming Clinton's well-greased machine is effective enough in each state to get her people to the polls for the primary, the general election will be fought in the nation at large, where right-wing media, local politicians and extreme churches have been fed and motivated for a generation on backlash politics, including Hillary hate. If there's one thing that scares people away from voting for her in battleground states like Montana or Nevada, it's the sense that she can't win because of the organized Right. Backlash groups, like Focus on the Family, Eagle Forum, and Concerned Women for America are organized and embedded in local churches and social groups, especially in rural districts, and they've been recruiting and backing candidates for years. They have fertile soil to draw on. "There are still ranters," says Theresa Kendrick of Montana Women Vote, a group that was instrumental in swinging the state for Governor Brian Schweitzer in 2004 and for Jon Tester, the tie-breaker in the Senate in 2006. "There are still plenty of people who say 'there's no way in hell I'm voting for a woman.'"[12]

Clinton is banking on the muscle of the middle: the corporate conservatives (like her new friend, media magnate Rupert Murdoch) who will ride on any party that preserves their profits, and the "invisible Americans," who would like to see a change but who aren't too involved in politics, and who like to think that middle-of-the-road politics won't impact their lives directly.

Clinton could win her party's nomination. She has an extraordinary ability to win supporters over. Even when their hearts lie with other candidates, Democratic voters seem inclined to back Hillary Clinton, in part because she's seen as the "toughest" candidate in the running. When she spoke at a Democratic contenders' forum held by AFSCME, the public workers' union in DC, the mostly low-income school and government workers liked Clinton's pledge to pass a Pay Nondiscrimination Act, but they erupted when Kucinich promised to repeal NAFTA on his first day in office. The crowd cheered Obama, Edwards, and Richardson more loudly and often than Clinton—but when interviewed afterwards, of half a dozen workers, all but one said she'd vote for Clinton. Ironically, for a campaign playing to women, Clinton wins because she's seen as the most macho. As person after person interviewed for this chapter put it, "She knows how to play hardball, and that's what you need in Washington." It's just possible there are enough of those kinds of voters to win Hillary Clinton the White House. The state of the organized Left in the US (and the devasting impact of the Bush/Cheney administration) is such that even Clinton's critics admit they're unlikely to sit out the general election. ("Ours is a reluctant love. Like an arranged marriage; she'll keep her side of the bargain but we may not be laughing all the way through dinner," says Catharine Stimpson, feminist author and Dean of Graduate Studies at New York University.) The provocation from the media keeps coming. In late July 2007, after she gave a speech on the Senate floor about the burdensome cost of higher education, the *Washington Post*'s staff writer Robin Givhan dedicated an entire column, not to her political plans, but to her cleavage: "There wasn't an unseemly amount of cleavage showing, but there it was. Undeniable."[13] Media sexism can probably be relied upon to fuel the ire of Clinton's fans, but the campaign season is long, and Clinton faces the challenge of keeping her supporters motivated.

As the organized Right has known for many years, in a narrowly divided country, the victory goes to the candidate whose ground troops not only vote, but dedicate themselves heart and soul to working for their candidate and turning every last voter out. Clinton has her fans, but her campaign stage is devoid of those who've done the most in the last few years to organize Americans to take action. There are no immigrant's rights leaders, no fair-trade advocates, and there is no trace, for obvious reasons, of the peace movement. There is no Mary Robinson on the stage, no Yanar Mohammed, head of the secular Iraqi women's movement, no Ann Wright or Cindy Sheehan. There can't be. As retired US army colonel and career foreign service officer Ann Wright put it, "Every minute Hillary's not bringing the troops home, I'm sitting her campaign out." Wright, who was Clinton's student at the University of Arkansas, knows something about sexism in big government institutions and she can't hide her pride at the idea of a woman in the White House. "I've waited my whole life," she says with a smile. But she's not going to work for Clinton unless something changes. "It's not just change in personnel I want in Washington, it's a change in policy," she says. Hearts have got to move in order for Clinton to become president. And those who have been moving hearts in the US are those from whom Hillary is—and always has been—at pains to keep her distance.

NOTES

1. Sarah Baxter, "Hillary Runs for the White House as 'new Thatcher,'" *The Sunday Times*, January 21, 2007.
2. Bill Schneider, CNN, March 19, 2007, Opinion Research Corp. Poll.
3. "Who's working Where," *The Sunday Monitor* (Concord) June 17, 2007, p.D3.
4. Hillary Clinton, *Living History*, Simon & Schuster, New York: 2003.
5. Gregg Sangillo, "Culture Wars and Silent Majorities," *The National Journal*, September 2, 2004.
6. Gail Sheehy, *Hillary's Choice*, Random House, New York: 1999, p. 194. Although she's barely mentioned in the reviews of the biographies that have followed, Sheehy's book did more original research than the subsequent biographies combined.
7. Sheehy, ibid, p. 345.
8. Sheehy, ibid, p. 194.
9. Peter Edelman, "The Worst Thing Bill Clinton Has Done," *The Atlantic Monthly,* March 1997.
10. Hillary Clinton, *Living History*, p. 365.
11. Katha Pollitt, "HRC: Can't Get No Respect," *The Nation*, November 20, 2006.

12. For more on the so-called Montana Miracle, see Laura Flanders, *Blue Grit: True Democrats Take Back Politics from the Politicians,* Penguin Press, New York: 2007.
13. Robin Givhan, "Hillary Clinton's Tentative Dip into New Neckline Territory," *Washington Post,* July 20, 2007, p. C01.

The Redeemer: Barack Obama

RICHARD GOLDSTEIN

JULY 2007. War. Terror. Tainted toothpaste and toys. A year remains before the presidential race gets real; a year of moral panics and manipulated crises, chaos called progress in Iraq, peril in Iran, and Pakistan. It is impossible to say how this season of doubt and dread will play out. But the major contradiction of the 2008 campaign is already in place.

By a large margin, people would rather see a Democrat in the White House. But when they are faced with the actual field of candidates, most voters choose a Republican—especially if Hillary Clinton runs. Whatever one may make of her predicament, it has given her campaign a risky edge. Her supporters know they may be aiding and abetting the enemy by nominating her, yet she is her party's front-runner. At this writing she holds a double-digit lead over her closest rival, Barack Obama.

But when independents are added to the mix, the race tightens. And when *all* likely voters are polled, Obama leads the pack. In fact, he is the only Democrat who beats the top-tier Republicans, including roaring Rudy and thrumming Fred. Here is the paradox that makes this campaign so tricky and so interesting. Democrats prefer Hillary, but Obama is down with the public. When voters are asked to choose the most inspiring candidate, his name comes up first.

In the end, he is far more likely to end up at the bottom of the ticket than at the top. That may explain why Obama has been so restrained around Clinton (though the gloves came off recently, when she called him naïve for promising to talk to the leaders of hostile nations). But there is a chance that he could rise from a brokered convention, following a primary season in which no candidate can claim a mandate; or that some scandal will penetrate Hillary's armor; or even that the Great Green Gore will deign to run, with Obama as his mate. It is too soon to foretell the fate of the junior senator from Illinois, the only African-American senator, and the only senator whose every quest—including his struggle to give up smoking—is part of the artfully woven tale he calls his "journey."

Call it packaging, call it hype. But that saga of personal and political discovery is the most exciting narrative to emerge from the Democratic repertoire in many years. It is not a drama of rising from meager expectations or a romance of courage under fire. Those are tropes of presidential theater, but Obama's story is a more like an epic that resounds with a root American theme: overcoming the burden of history.

For more than a decade, the triangulating folks at the Democratic Leadership Council (from whose loins Bill Clinton sprang) have been keening over their party's shrinking white male base. Carter was the last liberal liked by guys—and not for long. Ever since Reagan, this crucial constituency has been tacking to the right, and the Republicans have kept the course by playing to the anxieties of white men about their status in society. Flashpoint issues like abortion, gay rights, and even gun control are all inflected by the panic over patriarchal power, expertly cultivated by the Republicans. It has been very a very effective strategy. Only 37 percent of white men voted for John Kerry in 2004. But now there is a Democrat who stands a chance of straddling the gender gap as well as the racial divide. For reasons not entirely rational (but what *is* in presidential politics?), that man is Obama.

It must be a source of painful irony to the Clintonistas that he is the only candidate to successfully apply Bill's playbook. If Hillary were to crib one of Obama's signature lines—declaring, for example, that the country's biggest problem is not the budget deficit but "the empathy deficit"—it would seem focus-grouped rather than genuine, and she might seem like a sob sister, the last thing a female politician needs. Obama can make such slogans stick because they seem to emanate from his persona, and even his body. He has given triangulating a noble name by presenting it as reconciliation.

Obama has built so effectively on the Bill Clinton myth—right down to his appropriation of the word *hope*—and he has assembled around him so many veterans of the Clinton White House that he might as well be a product of the DLC, sent forth as an alternative brand in case Hillary should fail. Certainly his rise could not have occurred without the support of powerful factions in his party. These pros must have seen in him a man with a story so compelling that people might forget why they think of the Democrats as elite, effete, and way too sweet.

It was not just his speaking skills that landed Obama a

prime-time address at the 2004 Democratic Convention (the same event at which Kerry saluted from the podium and declared himself "reporting for duty"). It was not just Obama's negotiating skill that got him a seat on the Senate Foreign Relations Committee, which put him on a presidential track. It was his ability to animate the strategy of Democrats who believe that their popularity problem stems from their positions on the so-called social issues. These backlash-burned liberals would like to see the party subsume its commitment to women and minorities within a general appeal to "core values." Instead of addressing racism, sexism, or homophobia, just say *fairness*. All the leading Democratic contenders serve some version of this happy meal, but only Obama makes it go down smoothly. He may be a man of "profound decency, extraordinary smarts, and great eloquence," as Patricia J. Williams writes in *The Nation*. But the main reason why he makes fairness seem like something other than a sellout is that he speaks of it as a child of several continents, proclaiming in his writing and his witness: *E Pluribus Me*.

His struggle now is to evade the compliment that he has added verve and vigor to his party. Color, you might say— but not too much. One can, and should, speculate about whether a man of darker hue would have gotten so far, given the longer sentences meted out to criminals with blacker faces, or the deliberate darkening of O.J.'s face on the cover of *Time*. Still, Obama's skin is not what has made him a star. It is a less tangible quality, alluded to by Senator Joseph Biden when he called Obama "the first African American who's articulate and bright and clean and a nice-looking guy." Biden was scolded for that sentiment, if only because so many white people share it.

Obama is no Tiger Woods, the biracial golf champ who insists he isn't black but "Cablasian" (as in Caucasian, black, and Asian). Obama has no problem identifying himself as an African American—which he is, literally. But he is quick to insist, as he did on *60 Minutes*, that though he is "rooted in the African-American community, I am not defined by it." He leads with his mixed heritage, and that is a potent signifier. It summons an image of America without "all the bad stuff in our history," as the galumphing anchor Chris Matthews said recently. Every time Obama suggests that affirmative action should be phased out someday, or that it should be based on economic circumstance, he signals a future in which race is not the premise of identity. And he has only to open his mouth to close the deal. His affect is true to his middle-class roots and high educational level, yet it seems remarkable to many whites simply because it comes from a black man. Even more suspect, it feels like a cause for celebration. America the Beautiful. Where even a (n-word) can be president.

This self-congratulating sensation is the basis—though not the extent—of Obama's appeal to men and women alike. In place of panic, he evokes the ideal of racial healing. As a result he has the lowest negatives of any Democratic candidate. (Hillary has the highest.) Even some fundamentalists view him kindly, if only because the Christian Right has its own guilt to overcome. In a contest between Obama and a secularist like Giuliani, he could raid the Republican base in a way that Hillary Clinton never will. Such is the enduring power of race to generate unlikely alliances in American politics—and the great irony about Obama's campaign is that, though it is based on the ideal of a color-blind society, it is freighted by race.

He is the only Democrat whose presentation of spirituality, dipped but not drenched in black religious style, feels real enough to command respect from all sides. And, as a jock who doesn't have to set up a photo-op to sink a basket, he passes the buddy test. He does this even though he isn't macho in the classic sense. All sorts of problems arise from his mellow presentation of masculinity, but it is very much in keeping with the post–hip-hop style, which is animated rather than alienated, preppy rather than felonious, butch but not bitchifying.

There is a new masculine hero in entertainment. The crooner now competes with the thug. It is a stretch, but an irresistible one, to observe that Obama is the same body type as Justin Timberlake. He lacks the strut, but he is definitely bringing sexy back. And, like Spider Man, the superhero of the moment, he is less massive than fleet, less reflexive than reflective. This cultural style is one sign that the Bush administration has left a bitter taste in the mouth of machismo. The question is whether a crooner can seem presidential—and that is as important as the question of whether a black man can. After all, there have been several black presidents in the movies, all of them solidly patriarchal, thick of skin, deep of voice, and decisive. The black male body as Golem, a stone giant protecting the people.

It is one thing to savor this action-hero fantasy, quite another to actually elect a black man as president. We shall see, in the booth, what Obama's magic is worth. Still, 92 percent of Americans say they are willing to vote for a black candidate, up from 37 percent in 1958. This is not the sign of a color-blind society, but it may be evidence that race has taken on a heroic meaning.

Most white people do not react to Condoleezza Rice
the way they do to other cabinet members. There is something stirring about her, notwithstanding her politics. She
isn't just a talented woman who happens to be black; she
has the magic that is the curveball of stigma, a belief that
the pariah holds special and alluring powers. In the heroic
aspect of this stereotype, count the ebony athlete who is
undefeatable, the black sergeant who is merciless but fair,
the black star of your favorite interracial buddy film who
presides over the white star's manhood. This may be a
positive image, but it is still a flattened one, and grounded
in the mystique of race.

The line from Rice to Obama is evident. Both break the
black mold in a crucial respect. They are icons because of
the way they think—and we haven't had that kind of
black culture hero since Malcolm X and Martin Luther
King. But there the similarity ends. Rice's appeal, especially to conservatives, has much to do with her
unbending and assertive persona. Obama, by contrast, is
loose and laid back. These qualities usually denote a liberal, and his success is further proof of a new opening for
liberalism. Something similar happened in the early
1960s, when the Right seemed fossilized. Indeed, there
hasn't been a Democratic presidential candidate with such
positive charisma since the days of the Kennedys.

Obama cultivates the comparison with JFK (another
member of a formerly stigmatized group: Irish Catholics).
It is possible that such a magical leader will signify a
change in society broader than his platform would indicate. What Kennedy actually achieved was much less
important than the forces he unleashed, and the same
may true of Obama. He is an icon of so many American

dreams that he has only to move his long, lithe body and all eyes are on him.

You could see this magic at the United Church of Christ convention in Hartford, where Obama addressed a crowd of 10,000 delegates, most of them white. As he stood under the liberal Christian slogan "God is Still Speaking," a multitude of hands flew up and fluttered in his direction. It was a traditional gesture of communion, but it came with squeals and shrieks not usually heard at this assembly. He looked tired. The lines in his face were deeper than they seem on television, and his eyes were hooded with fatigue. He spoke over his applause, hurrying the speech along, and he left when it was over, with barely a wave. But it didn't matter. The crowd was transported by his presence. The preacherly touches in his delivery were apparent but restrained, as were the subtle tributes to black rhetorical style—the rising cadences and swooping lilts, held in check by his flat Midwestern tone. There was nothing about his delivery to trigger the racial panic that threatens to erupt from the hidden depths of even many liberal whites when a black man seems too "black."

This racial balancing act is hardly unknown to black professionals, but for Obama-it is not just a campaign strategy. It is the product of a lifelong struggle, vividly described in his memoir *Dreams From My Father*. He grew up with the acute awareness that, in order to fulfill the ambitions of his white Midwestern mom and his equally ambitious Kenyan dad, he would have to resist the usual project of young black men: locating and affirming their manhood in the culture of the hoop and the street. He poured his energy into the former, becoming a fiercely competitive basketball player, but he merely dabbled in the latter, settling for the occasional snort and drunk. All along, he understood that it was possible to impress white people simply by being polite, but this etiquette required an enormous repression of feeling.

If Hillary must project strength without sparking male panic—a tricky mission, to be sure—Obama must modulate the various elements in his racial identity to present a picture that is both authentic and anodyne. This is the task of every stigmatized individual, but when a black man performs it successfully the effect is exhilarating for white people, and you could see that at the UCC convention. It almost didn't matter what he said (though he hit the right notes with this crowd, accusing the Right of "hijacking faith"). He could have been lip-synching an old Sam Cooke ballad and the fans would have roared anyway. In fact, he did sound a bit like Cooke's mellow civil-rights anthem of the '60s, "A Change is Gonna Come."

He is no Sojourner Truth, ready to bare a breast to her stunned white audience in a paroxysm of freedom preaching. His speeches are interesting mostly because of their absence of fight lines. They bear about the same relationship to his writing as greeting-card verse does to poetry. There is a fondness for the carefully navigated bromide, a gift for the soothing cliché. And his delivery seems calculated to produce a mildly sedating effect. If you stay alert you will hear a reasoned argument well within the parameters of the Democratic mainstream, softened by a warm demeanor and cut with a nod to God. Seasoned pundits

are confused by this mellow tendency, reading it as hesi-
tance or even timidity. He is "tentative about commanding
the stage and consistently channeling the excitement he
engenders," writes *New York Times* columnist Maureen
Dowd, Obama's severest critic in the media (and one of
Hillary's biggest fans). "When he should fire up, he damp-
ens. When he should dominate, he's deferential."

This low-burner style is intended to "show people how
I think," Obama insists. But it has the effect of forcing
you to watch his body. As your attention flags, all sorts of
associations are free to operate. And when you see him—
that be-my-baby face, that firm physique (starring the
tightest butt in politics), that beatific grin—you want to
watch him for four more years. He claims to be distressed
by the idolatry, griping to *New York Times* columnist
Frank Rich about how "difficult it is to break through the
interest in me on the beach." Still, no one forced him to
pose for *GQ* and *Men's Vogue*. Beauty is not truth, especially in politics, but glamour of the sort that celebrities
radiate is more than just a matter of buff or babeitude. It
is the sign of something that the Christians who basked in
his thrall at the UCC convention might call grace.

Hillary Clinton has a strong persona, but if she wins, it
will not be because of charisma. She lacks the magic that
seems bestowed on the chosen one. Every time she tries to
project magnetism, her deep investment in physical
restraint becomes apparent. She is hemmed in by the need
to repress the erotic side, which could prove threatening.
(Consider the media storm that followed her appearance on
the Senate floor in an outfit that actually showed décol-
letage.) Or perhaps she is temperamentally unable to play
the glamour card. In any case, she does not do alluring, pre-

ferring to let her plumpish body and her self-deprecating turns—as in singing the national anthem off-key—convey charm. But Obama has no need for indirection. He is free to encourage desire in all its ramifications, and expert at tapping the utopian thinking that has been driven out of politics by terror and its exploitation. No other candidate is as adept at signaling change without proposing it.

Of course, the odds have always been with Hillary. Obama cannot match her crack organization on the ground, or her call on endorsements from politicians in debt to the party aparat. Yet he has done astonishingly well at fundraising, outpacing Clinton's bundling machine and assembling an unprecedented base of about 250,000 donors. The announcement of that feat, just before the July 4 weekend, lifted the Obama campaign from the funk of second place and certified him as a serious contender— the only one who can claim a grassroots movement at his back. In fact, only about a third of his cash comes from small donors; fat cats provide the rest. Still, no candidate has come close to the breadth of his support; in part because none of them can match his crack Internet operation, run by the founder of Facebook, an immensely popular website with the young. No wonder he leads all the candidates from both parties among voters under thirty.

Clinton's smaller donor base means that she will have to call on the same people over and over in order to keep up with the cash flow from Obama's vast pool of contributors. As a result, he may actually outspend her in the long run. It would be foolish to underestimate Clinton's access to deep Democratic pockets (notwithstanding a few highly publicized defections in Hollywood). She has the chits, but Obama has the newcomers, the gatecrashers, the young in age and opportunity. He has managed to cultivate a cadre of black executives at major corporations and hedge-fund wizards who feel shut out of their place at the patronage table. California is his biggest money state, but he has been unexpectedly successful in New York City, Clinton's metropol. And he has benefited from the growing pool of black business celebrities, such as hip-hop magnate Russell Simmons and Sheila C. Johnson, the co-founder of Black Entertainment Television. Their passion for his candidacy is different from the dutiful support Clinton has garnered in the black community. She has the blessing of Maya Angelou, the designated poet of her husband's inauguration—but Obama has Oprah.

He also has the ghost of Harold Washington, who emerged from one of the most racist campaigns in recent American history to become the first black mayor of Chicago in 1983. Obama's closest political advisor, David Axelrod, worked on Washington's re-election campaign, and last year he managed the campaign of Deval Patrick, the first black governor of Massachusetts (where African Americans are only 6 percent of the population). Patrick's ads often included lingering shots of Obama listening attentively. The connection is not incidental: both men are part of a new generation of leaders drawn from a black professional class that can afford to dream big. What has changed for this elite, Obama writes in his most recent book, *The Audacity of Hope*, is "their rejection of any limits to what they can achieve"—and that, he notes, is "a radical break from the past." He is the emblem of this new unfettering. Hence, the slogan devised by Alexrod for Obama's US Senate campaign: "Yes we can."

Sammy Davis Jr. chose a similar motto for his autobiography, *Yes I Can*. That was in 1965. So perhaps the sense of limitless potential that Obama describes is not really a new attitude but the response to a new situation. Though its wealth is still relatively modest, the black aspirational elite is far more visible in the white world, and now Obama has put this class on the political map. For the first time, there is a real battle for their money and their votes, at least among Democrats. Republicans are more likely to show up at a same-sex wedding than at an event sponsored by the NAACP. (Its recent presidential forum drew only one Republican, the immigrant-bashing Tom Tancredo.) But this fall all the GOP candidates will appear at a Howard University debate modeled on the one for Democrats that took place in June, broadcast by PBS. It was a remarkable national event, if only because the moderator, Tavis Smiley, and most of the questioners were black.

Hillary Clinton was afire, especially when she was asked about the AIDS crisis. "If HIV/AIDS was the leading cause of death of white women between the ages of twenty-one and thirty-four, there would be an outrage in this country," she proclaimed to a thunderous ovation. It was a well-tailored remark, cut on the bias in just the right way. Obama was less bold, walking a careful line between progressive rhetoric and self-improvement sermonizing. He spoke of the need for both personal and social responsibility in combating AIDS. Clinton established her credentials, but Obama went after something subtler by emphasizing the connection between his audience and himself. As in: "We need someone in the White House who will recognize our children as his own." He is the only candidate who can say *you* and *I* to a black crowd without sounding at least a little strained. This affinity is proving more persuasive than the doubts about his fidelity to the community. At one point in the Howard debate, the camera picked up the prominent black intellectual Cornel West. Once he had blasted Obama for holding African Americans "at arm's length" in order to reach whites. But after a phone call from the candidate he enlisted as an unpaid advisor, and now he was shouting "O-Ba-Ma!" with his arm pumping a power salute.

There was another famous face in the crowd at Howard. Al Sharpton looked dour when the camera caught him, as if he were attending a reception for his old foe Giuliani. Sharpton has been Obama's most vocal black critic, a stance that surely has to do with his status as an (occasional) Friend of Hillary. But, as is usually the case with Sharpton, there is substance along with self-interest in his critique. To say that Obama never experienced the effects of slavery—or even to suggest, as some reports have, that his ancestors on his mother's side actually owned slaves—is a loaded way of raising the issue that has haunted him in the black community: his privilege, as a multiracial child raised in a white household, and the perspective that might bring. As Sharpton put it: "Just because you are our color doesn't mean you are our kind."

Obama's work as a community organizer has blunted this charge, but it remains the case that he does not speak Homey. Nor does he represent the populist stream in black political thought, as Sharpton does. The word *struggle* rarely appears in his speeches, and there is no hint of the street smarts that animate Sharpton's remarks. The closest Obama gets to that tradition is alluding to Cousin

Pookie, the layabout who is a staple on the black comedy circuit. As in: "If Cousin Pookie would get off his butt and vote . . ."

Obama is more comfortable sounding churched, though that, too, is something he has had to learn. He grew up with a broad skeptical streak, but when he discovered that it was hard to organize poor people without sharing their faith he joined a congregation. Now he campaigns assiduously in black churches, delivering speeches that often focus on fatherhood and family. The black ministers he praises are not the likes of Jesse Jackson (who has been much kinder to him than Sharpton has), but preachers of personal uplift such as the Reverend T. D. Jakes, whom he calls "a friend." Karl Rove would probably agree, since he has cited Jakes as "a vital partner" in the GOP's effort to court blacks. It is easy to see why this opportunistic flexibility would rile Sharpton, if only because Obama does it so much better. But also because it repudiates a progressive standard: The whole community must rise, not just its exceptional members.

The conflict between strategies of uplift and agitation has raged in black society since the nineteenth century. The new aspirational class has synthesized both approaches, but their experience tracks them toward the option of self-betterment. This leaves a protest-oriented leader like Sharpton with a hard lesson to learn, though it is one all activists must eventually face. If your ideas are shared by the next generation, it will mean that you have failed, because the world remains the same. But if you succeed you will be bypassed, because the world has changed.

Obama is the face of these emerging circumstances. He is the black man from hope—and does he ever flog that mantra! His PAC is called Hopefund, and his speeches are larded with the h-word. In another mouth it would sound like a cliché, but from Obama it resonates in a special way, as do his constant references to empathy. "I think I have the capacity to get people to recognize themselves in each other," he told ABC's George Stephanopoulis. Like so much else about Obama's appeal, the truth is less heart-warming but more profound.

There is a new racial etiquette in America, an air of casualness, especially among the young. But it masks the threat of mortification if the tautly drawn lines are crossed. Every time a white celebrity gets caught in a *macaca* moment, it is both a repudiation of racism and a recognition that this sin still lurks under the reformed surface. With that knowledge comes the weight of one's secret perceptions. For whites who are honest about the echoes of racism that still call out, there is an intense desire to be free of the contradiction between feeling and intention. Without ever saying so, and perhaps without meaning to, Obama plays to this yearning.

There is no way for him to address that emotion—it would be far too disturbing. So he relies on platitudes that reverberate, as his appearance does, with unspoken expectations. At his most rote he sounds like a motivational speaker without a product. "Obama-speak," the leftist writer Alexander Cockburn calls it; "a pulp of boosterism about the American dream." And that message doesn't necessarily fly with those who need hope most. As you go down the income and educational scales you find less support for Obama, among blacks and whites alike. And among Latinos, the most important new Democratic constituency, Hillary is *manos*-down the favorite. This is one reason why she leads Obama in the West. Indeed, as of July 4, she was the frontrunner in every early primary state except South Carolina, with its large black Democratic electorate. It would take a major shift to confound these polls, but other candidates have come from behind on the strength of a far less significant story.

No politician in our time has a more compelling identity résumé, as delineated in *Dreams from My Father*. If nothing else, this deeply affecting book, published in 1995, when he was beginning to consider running for office, positions Obama as the most literary politician since . . . since when? (He is also the first presidential candidate to win a Grammy, for his recording of the book. No wonder Cornel West, the only scholar to record a rap record, is a fan.)

As an image-building tool, *Dreams from My Father* has been remarkably effective. But it is too unorthodox to serve as a press release. Not only are there damning references to coke sniffing and dope smoking—when asked recently if he inhaled, Obama jauntily replied, "That was the point!"—but the book also offers a detailed account of his gnawing ambivalence as a young man growing up in a double bind. When he embarks for Kenya to meet his African family he sees himself as "a Westerner not entirely at home in the West, an African on his way to a land full of strangers. . . . I felt as if I were living out someone else's romance."

He was still known as Barry when his father visited him briefly, at the age of ten. In school, he made up Disneyesque stories about his Kenyan tribe to ward off the tittering of his white peers. He remembers seeing a picture of a black man who tried to peel off his skin and deducing from the photo that "there was a hidden enemy out there, one that could reach me without anyone's knowledge, not even my own." He mastered the task of maintaining a decorum that had the sole purpose of disarming the anxieties of white students. It would serve him well at Harvard (where his nickname was Baroque Yo-Mama) and later as a politician, but it would also keep him at a distance from black culture, aggravating his alienation and perhaps stopping him from being more active in the civil rights movement. In the book he fudges the issue of his political quiescence, and he lets his hoop buddy Ray express the anguish of his situation: "Being black meant only the knowledge of your own powerlessness, of your own defeat. Should you refuse this defeat and lash out at your captors, they would have a name for that, too, a name that could cage you just as good. Paranoid. Militant. Violent. Nigger."

One can only imagine how the intensely managed self-control that Obama is known for grew out of this painful sensitivity to manners, and how he turned the resentment he felt every time he had to pose as a not-angry black man into a political skill. But his loving relationship with his white mother and her parents makes the comfort he displays and inspires in whites feel genuine. It is the bedrock of his ability to cross over, and by now it has become an ability to connect across *all* lines, including ideological ones.

His image, so skillfully burnished, has cracked a bit under pressure. He has suffered several embarrassing stumbles, including a dirty-tricks memo on Clinton that backfired because it sought to foment scandal in her dealings with Indian-American businessmen involved in outsourcing. (The memo referred to Clinton as the Democrat from Punjab, an unconscionable hit from this man of many nations.) He has a tendency, at such moments, to apologize and move on, letting the original impression stick. More fatefully, he has yet to find a way to turn his Ambien style into the sharply honed delivery that is suitable for a televised debate. But like the Energizer Bunny, he keeps going and going. And what a gnash it must be for Hillary to realize that he is the most charming Democrat since her husband Bill.

He certainly is not a man of the Left. As Alexander Cockburn points out, Obama gave money to Joseph Lieberman during his battle with progressive Ned Lamont (though, when Lamont won the Democratic primary, Obama endorsed him). He has a penchant for turning his back on progressives, and in 2000 he ran for the Congress against a former Black Panther—and lost. As a US senator, he supported tort reform, voted against filibustering the nomination of Samuel Alito to the Supreme Court (where this Justice joined the new majority in gutting affirmative action), and backed the USA PATRIOT Improvement and Reauthorization Act. He favors capital punishment (though only in cases of "heinous" crime). He calls himself a strong supporter of reproductive rights, but in the Illinois legislature he voted *present* instead of *yea* on a number of bills concerning parental notification and late-term abortion. On the stump now, he shies away from "social issues" unless he is speaking to a crowd that expects him to comment, and he can be very forgiving of social conservatives such as Reverend Jakes, who has called homosexuality a "brokenness."

There is another minister in Obama's life, the Reverend Jeremiah Wright, who leads a black superchurch in Chicago. That was the congregation Obama joined as a young organizer. It had a great influence on him, and so did Wright. One of his sermons, "The Audacity of Hope," gave Obama the title of his second book (much less interesting than the first, showing signs of the stylization that would sand the texture from his prose). When Obama was ready to announce for president, Wright was set to deliver the invocation. "Fifteen minutes before *shabos*," he told the *New York Times*, "I got a call from Barack. One of his members had talked him into uninviting me."

It was a defining moment—one of many in which Obama chose the lucrative (he might say productive) alternative to radical politics. For Wright had once paid a visit to Muammar Khadafi, and his church had begun as an Afrocentric congregation. It isn't hard to imagine what the media meat machine would have made of these associations. Obama did what he had to do in order to get over. In the end, Wright could not count on his loyalty.

As an activist in Chicago, Obama respected Black Nationalists—he had to—but he rejected their project, finding it parochial and unsuitable to his temperament. Unsuitable also to the role he felt suited for in life. But who can blame him? He did not know radical activism in its heyday; he grew up as the Left, battered by factionalism and police-perpetrated assassination, retreated to the academy. That is why he can get away with describing radical politics as "old grudges and revenge plots hatched out on a handful of college campuses long ago." He has an unerring instinct for avoiding the Left because he is aware of its failure—and he is not about to risk a vote for a vanquished vision.

"I have a curious relationship to the Sixties," Obama writes. They made him but also constrained him. He has complained that "the narrative of black politics is still shaped by the Sixties and black power." Yet, for all that he flees from that damned decade, his prospects are ultimately tied to its gist and jive. The '60s produced the identity politics Obama decries, but they were also a time when transracialism became a driving force, especially among the young. This was the spark that gave the counterculture its funky fire. It heats Obama now.

At the heart of transracialism is the need for redemption; not just relief from guilt, but deliverance from the corrupting and constricting structures that racism creates. In the '60s, this concept was widely regarded as the key to freeing up all sorts of blocked energy. (For example, smashing the racial order invited an attack on the sexual order.) New laws were needed for justice to prevail, but in order for liberation to occur there would have to be a real meeting of the races. Desire would be unleashed; the lust for the other that had been shaped—and suppressed—by bigotry. Sometimes this passion took the form of sex, but it also fueled everything from the blast of rock to the joy of marching together for civil rights. (See the musical *Hairspray* for a retro look at this empowering vision.) And it wasn't just a personal high. Transracialism was about realizing our national destiny. Kick out the jams and a new, ecstatic democracy would grow.

Certainly this is a myth, but myths are not untrue—only unreal. And the belief that racial fusion will form a more perfect union is not just a '60s fantasia. It is deeply encoded in American culture. It informs the intense physicality of Ishmael's bond with Quequeg, and the passion of Nigger Jim for Huck Finn; it hovers over the rhapsodic mixing in *Showboat*, over Chuck Berry's lewd invitations and Eminem's shady spew. Even the cartoon feature *Ratatouille*, in which an upwardly mobile rat teaches a human how to cook, can be read as a transracial parable. That is how deeply the longing for absolution from America's Original Sin cuts in our art and entertainment. Obama bristles at the idea that his campaign represents "an easy shortcut to racial reconciliation." But the dream remains. It is the source of his grace—and the reason why he is hot.

It isn't just his well-worked lats, or the suits that David Letterman called "electable." (Did he really want to say *delectable*?) Obama taps the erotic energy of transracialism. Just ask the undulating vixen with the eyes of Ronnie Spector, circa The Ronettes, who calls herself Obama Girl. Her YouTube video "I Got a Crush on Obama" has made her a true fifteen-minute sensation—and that might have been the point, since she told one interviewer that she hadn't actually decided whether to vote for her man. It may be that she was retained by the same whiz kids in Obama's camp who designed the viral video that placed Hillary Clinton in a grim 1984 setting. Who can say? But whatever her provenance, Obama Girl has her laminated nails on the pulse of America, as she gleefully sings, "You're into border security/Let's break this border between you and me." Inserting herself into a pec-ful photo of the O-Man in his swimming trunks, she declares: "You're a lover who can fight/You can roar with me tonight."

As the old blues song has it: "The men don't know, but

the little girls understand." The question is never whether sex is absent from an election, but whether the race hinges on embracing or fleeing from sexuality. With Obama, Eros is front and center whether he likes it or not, because his aura is shaped by the ecstasy that American culture attaches to the dream of fusion between blacks and whites. This is a mystique that inspires assassination, and it's no surprise that Obama was the first of this year's candidates to receive secret-service protection. (Hillary already had it, since she is a former First Lady.) His Senate colleague Dick Durbin says that this precaution had "everything to do with race," and there have been unspecified reports of threats on Obama's life. But perhaps the danger he is in has less to do with his pedigree than with the promise that killed the Kennedys. The promise of transformation.

The ability to inspire devotion, to infuse a vision with the magic of one's persona and thereby to shape a nation—Americans have an almost innocent trust in this quality, and a mistrust of politicians who don't project its heart-thumping aura. In a recent study, people viewed silent clips of unfamiliar politicians, and, without hearing the content of their speeches, these people were able to pick the winner of nearly every race. Charisma shows before it tells. But it takes more than a compelling persona to stir the passions; more than a regally aloof air, a personal saga that involves the overcoming of an ordeal, a touch of the exotic, a diffident edge and a humanizing flaw (smoking, in Obama's case). These are the traits sociologists associate with charisma. But one more thing is essential: A leader with grace must embody the current under the surface of ordinary life, the underground spring of a culture's most potent yearnings. If Obama is a charismatic figure, it is because, beneath his measured articulations, he evokes what Norman Mailer has called "the dreamlife of America."

Here is Mailer on JFK during the 1960 campaign: "This candidate, for all his record, his good, sound, liberal record, has a patina of that other life, the second American life, the long electric night with the fires of neon leading down the highway to the murmur of jazz." Obama does not hit those notes, for jazz is no longer the music of the dreamlife, and the fires of neon have given way to the low-rez glow of MySpace. But he is the current conjurer of the dreamlife. He is the representing one.

That may explain why Obama isn't more popular in his party. Charisma is a curse among Democrats. They share a conviction that grace is dangerous, that politicians who shape an agenda by dint of their personae are inevitably duplicitous, that the neon fires are best confined to song and dance. This fear of the primal is not just a reaction to the party's lingering association with the let-it-all-hang-out. It is the sign of a more fundamental problem: the inclination to choose candidates who fit into the party machinery rather than strong individuals who make their own way. Reagan taught Republicans to value the charismatic outsider, but that is a concept Democrats have yet to understand. They cling to the belief that elections are won by appealing to interests rather than feelings. This is a futile strategy, as Drew Westin demonstrates in his new book, *The Political Brain*. To think that a psychologist could make a splash by urging Democrats to study the emotional makeup of human beings. Any marketer could have told them that.

The manipulation of emotion is the basis of selling—has been ever since Edward Bernays, the founder of public relations, enlisted the ideas of his uncle Sigmund Freud. In the 1920s, Bernays convinced women to buy cake mix by getting the manufacturer to require the addition of an unnecessary egg. ("A gift from the womb," he called it.) In the 1950s, he supplied the alibis that allowed Eisenhower to justify his interventions in Central America. Ever since Reagan, the Republicans have run with Bernays's theories like the vulgar Freudians they are, demonizing their opponents and stoking identification with their candidates. The Democrats respond like the rationalists they are, or, even worse, they weave clumsy narratives that don't play in the cineplex of the mind. They lack what scholar and activist Stephen Duncombe calls "dreampolitik."

In his prescient book, *Dream: Re-Imagining Progressive Politics in an Age of Fantasy,* Duncombe urges the Left to create a spectacle that reflects its own values, one that "breaks down hierarchies, fosters community, allows for diversity, and engages with reality while asking what new realities might be possible." That is the pageant Obama has fashioned. He may not be a prog, but he has figured out how to trigger the primal without tapping the sadomasochistic needs that make authoritarians seem like saviors. He knows it isn't just faith that the Right has hijacked; it is fantasy.

The reverie he evokes may be the only one that can compete with the myth of danger and deliverance that keeps the strongman in business. For this dream of racial redemption is powerful, not just because it is imbedded in the culture, but because it elides with a religious ideal: America the Light Unto Nations, the new, improved Jerusalem. Obama's achievement is to take this myth of destiny and apply it to the conditions of the present. He embodies two dynamic intersecting forces: black aspiration and white expiation—and that is a very heady mix.

★ ★ ★

The webzine *Slate* has begun an "Obama Messiah Watch." They have a point. Let us presume we are electing a president, not a savior.

What kind of leader would Obama be? He is far less defined by his statements—and his record—than Hillary Clinton is. That, too, is part of his charisma: Mailer says of Kennedy, "He is not in focus." Obama hasn't covered his tracks, but he has made it hard to find them under the ornamental shrubbery. His footprints lead to the conclusion that caution and synthesis would be his standard operating procedure.

You can see these tendencies in Obama's healthcare plan, which bars insurers from refusing coverage to anyone, lets people choose between private plans and a public one, and offers subsidies to those who cannot afford the rates. This approach borrows heavily from John Edwards's much-praised scheme, but it falls short of his call for universal coverage. At any rate, *The New Republic* estimates that Obama's plan would leave about fifteen million American uninsured. *New York Times* columnist Paul Krugman calls this "the timidity of hope."

It can be argued that an incremental attitude is the best way to pass liberal legislation these days. Obama has said as much. "For a political leader to get things done, he or she ideally should be ahead of the curve, but not too far ahead," he told Ken Silverstein of *Harper's*. With a securely Democratic Congress at his back, Obama might be bolder. But there is nothing in his record that augurs real audacity. And his advisers—mostly drawn from the Clinton White House and the Kennedy School of Government—are careful liberal types. The best that can be said of them is that they are not Henry Kissinger.

Much was made of Obama's "briefing" by Colin Powell, read as a signal that he would be open to input from Republicans. Indeed, his closet ally on the Senate Foreign Relations Committee is Republican Richard Lugar. Obama is known as a liberal who can connect with conservatives. Perhaps that is because he is accommodating as well as charming. To judge from the agenda that appears on his website, Obama would drive down the center lane with a slight veer to the left. For example, he would rebuild the military, launch a global effort to stop nuclear proliferation, and strengthen impoverished countries. There is no critique of the military-industrial complex in his pitch, only a general statement about leading the world "by deed and example." A critic might say: Sounds like Jimmy Carter on a good day. A supporter might counter: That would be a real improvement over the predatory style of American foreign policy now. And they both would be right.

On the crucial question of Iraq, Obama has been fairly active in the Senate. He introduced a bill to begin troop redeployment in May of 2007 (it failed, as he must have known it would), but he has been critical of Representative John Murtha's calls for a quick withdrawal. Again, that strategy: tacking slightly to the left while attacking the Left to make his position seem centrist. He was an early critic of the Iraq invasion, and in the most recent vote to cut off funding for the war he voted *yes*, but only at the last minute and without comment, following Hillary's lead.

It remains to be seen whether a President Obama could work the magic on Republicans that he did in the Illinois legislature, where he was credited with building bipartisan support for a bill that deterred racial profiling. As a state senator, he helped to devise an ambitious ethics reform, led a drive to define healthcare as a basic human right (it failed to pass), worked to expand early-childhood education, and played a part in making Illinois the first state to require taping of police interrogations. He built a reputation as an advocate for the poor, and, while he has not abandoned that role, neither has he run on it. That would be Edwards.

One unasked question is whether Obama would follow policies that might be called Afrocentric. Any attempt to pass legislation that benefits the underclass could be viewed this way, as could any foreign policy that sees America as one spoke among many on the wheel of the world. Given the pressure he would be under, it is possible that he would steer clear of such an agenda—and even covet criticism from the likes of Sharpton. Perhaps the real test is whether his biography will influence his position on issues like trade favoritism and debt forgiving. So far, he does not seem eager to pose with Bono.

He certainly would project a new American profile across the world. His father was Muslim, albeit "a reluctant Muslim," following the custom of his Kenyan village, Obama writes. During his boyhood years in Indonesia, he attended a Muslim school (not a madrassa, as the fright rumor claims), and his teacher wrote his mother to complain that he made faces during Koranic readings. But he had the audacity to sing the Muslim call to prayer to *New York Times* columnist Nicholas Kristoff, calling it "one of the prettiest sounds on Earth at sunset." The shock jocks have already begun to make hay of his surname, dubbing him Osama—and never mind his middle name, Hussein. One can expect the strings of American xenophobia to be lavishly plucked if he takes center stage.

To his credit, he hasn't responded with a show of compensatory bellicosity, but neither does he fly like a dove. "I don't oppose all wars," he said at a peace rally in 1992. "What I am opposed to is a dumb war. What I am opposed to is a rash war." This is hardly an ethical stance. Still, who can say what difference it would make to have a president who knows the night-runner legends of his African tribe and remembers wishing, when he received his letter of acceptance to Harvard, that he was back in Indonesia "running barefoot along a paddy field, with my feet sinking into the cool, wet mud, part of a chain of other brown boys chasing after a tattered kite."

This ambivalence toward power—a running thread in his writing—has not stopped him from engineering the most unlikely rise in national politics since Wendel Wilkie came out of nowhere to run against Roosevelt in 1940. Obama has been lucky in his opponents. He campaigned for the US Senate against one Republican who became mired in a sex scandal, and another (gadfly Alan Keyes) whose conservatism wouldn't play in Barry Goldwater's breakfast nook, much less in Chicago.

That city is notorious for its corrupt politics, and, despite his goo-goo professions, Obama hasn't entirely avoided the web of interlocking interests. His longtime relationship with a Syrian-born realtor, Antoin Rezko, has dented his image. Rezko, now under federal indictment for favor trading and fraud, was one of Obama's first funders, and over the years he contributed about $150,000 to Obama's various campaigns. Obama's law firm represented Rezko, and as a state legislator he recommended the developer for state housing grants that netted Rezko and a partner $855,000 in fees. Obama didn't seem to notice that a number of Rezko buildings in his low-income district failed. Nor did he consider that Rezko was under investigation when he allowed the developer's wife to sell him an adjacent plot of land that enlarged the lawn on his newly purchased $1.65 million suburban home. He has given all the Rezko money currently in his larder to charity, and he has called the land deal "boneheaded," putting it down to anxieties about purchasing a first home (though his family had previously lived in a Hyde Park condo). No one has alleged that Obama did anything illegal, but his slip-sliding response to questions about Rezko suggests that, should he succeed, he will not drive every pig from the trough.

Though his campaign brags that it hasn't taken money from lobbyists or PACs, that is not exactly true—nor was it the case during Obama's previous campaigns. His war chest has included money from industry councils, which are akin to PACs. Exelon, the nation's largest nuclear-power plant operator, has been a significant donor, as have brokerage giants such as Goldman Sachs, Morgan Stanley, and Citigroup. Then there are the bundlers, who harvest contributions from individuals into a large, lump sum. In Obama's case, that includes several individuals who are federal lobbyists, and others who work at law firms or run businesses that hire lobbyists. These are not the grassroots he boasts about; they are entities with a vital interest in things like energy, trade, and social-security funds. And while he has not been a mouthpiece for his donors, neither has he been indifferent to their needs.

In the state senate he helped to defeat an amendment that would have stopped vast loan guarantees to power-plant operators that undertake new energy projects, and he voted *against* capping credit-card interest rates. His friends at Exelon and Citibank must have been pleased. And his buds at the Illinois soybean and corn growers associations surely noticed his rabid support for ethanol. He is not especially greedy or corrupt, as politicians go. But that, say his critics, is the point. He is, finally, like other politicians.

☆ ☆ ☆

When you scour the media for dirt on Obama, hypocrisy is not what pops up. Nor does triangulation, unless one reads the progressive press. First and foremost, his detractors see him as a kid, which he is not. At forty-five, Obama is two years *older* than JFK was when he ran for president, but he is widely regarded as too inexperienced to play the crucial role of commander in chief. The conservative commentator George Will writes that Obama would make the presidency "an entry level position." To which he has replied: "Nobody had better Washington experience than Dick Cheney or Donald Rumsfeld. If the criterion is how long you've been in Washington, then we should just go ahead and assign Joe Biden or Chris Dodd the nomination."

Obama does give a youthful impression. He hasn't fully shaken off his prep-school yearbook photo, which shows him aa gangly Afro-sporting kid who could have been a member of the Jackson Family. But one cannot rule out the possibility that the experience issue is inflected by the anxieties that surround the thought of a black man becoming the most powerful person on Earth. After all, no one calls Giuliani green, though his foreign policy experience consists entirely of throwing Yasir Arafat out of Lincoln Center. Abraham Lincoln had an even skimpier résumé than Obama's when he ran for president on the (newly constituted) Republican line. Of course, Lincoln did not have the ears of a faun.

Every time Obama advances a conciliatory idea it conspires with his juvenile appearance, and his deliberative streak can seem like indecisiveness. The word cropping up in the media, now that the breathy praise which greeted Obama's arrival has turned to snarking, is *squishy*. At a time when many Democrats are terrified of seeming soft, this could be the diss of death. Especially in the charged arena of TV debates, where an attack quip delivered with a smiling face is the signifier of a well-honed brutal streak. Here, Obama's ruminative style makes him seem like a lover without the thrust of dominance. He is not "manned up." Is that why he does not seem presidential? If we imagine that machismo is the mark of leadership, we will be electing Republicans forever.

Obama's problem is not actually a lack of aggression but a frantic grasping for the center. He can be plenty pushy when facing a rival on his left. In the first South Carolina debate, he pounded Edwards for voting to authorize the Iraq War in 2002, but he didn't even graze Clinton, who had made the same mistake. In fact, he gave her an opening to show hard. Asked what he would do if two American cities came under attack, Obama answered that the first response should be to see that an effective emergency team is in place. Hillary spoke of retaliation.

You run a *Kumbaya* moment at your risk, as she knows—
and as Obama discovered when the reviews came in.
"O'Bambi." That was Maureen Dowd's judgment—
harsh but not unusually so, for her. Then she slipped into
the swamp, dubbing Obama "The Boy Wonder." In subsequent columns she would change that phrase to "First
Lad," showing some residual sensitivity, but this was her
Joe Biden moment. Just as he had exposed his innards by
calling Obama "clean"—as if scrubbed of dark and dirty
stuff—she had made a similar slip. *Boy Wonder* is not a
racist remark by intention, but Obama sets off the white
subconscious, resulting in all sorts of odd blurtations. And
he is hardly unique in that respect. Black politicians are
often tarred by indirection. In 2006, the Democratic sen-
atorial candidate from Tennessee, a black man, fell victim
to an attack ad featuring a scantily clad white woman and
the tag line: "Harold Ford. He's not right!" Churn that
slogan through the mind, let it tickle the neurons of prim-
itive association, and a telling variation emerges: *Harold
Ford. He's not white.*

It is unfashionable, in the mainstream media, to decon-
struct too deeply, to probe a seemingly innocent statement
for its hidden social implications. But racializing is realizing. So, what does it mean when a leading columnist labels
Obama a boy wonder? Like the complaint about his inex-
perience, this one may be valid, but it is also racially
inflected. He does not meet the model of the African-
American warrior. He is not a rock; he is a thinking reed.
And, in a culture still enchanted by the dichotomy between
the black body and the white mind (see Spike Lee's film
Bamboozled), Obama's pensive presentation can raise anxieties even as it soothes them. A black hero must have a

basso profundo and a physique of pumped iron. Obama lacks these attributes. He doesn't fit the myth, so how can he be the Man? Why, he isn't even a *real* man! He is "squishy."

Setting out to reassure, Obama reveals that race is still a primary concept, even among those who are not bigots, and even for white folks who bask in his gaze. After all, isn't it racist to expect a black man to redeem America? And isn't it foolish?

Yes. But still, there is the dream.

I know what it is like to interview a presidential candidate on the hoof. As a reporter, I followed Bill Clinton through the Midwest during the 1992 campaign. In the ninety seconds it took him to walk from a hotel lobby to a bus, he gave me a great quote. I felt blessed—until I discovered later that the same line had appeared in countless stories.

I didn't want to play that game with Obama. I wanted to stand back and watch him in a relatively unscripted event, the way I had seen Clinton descend on a strip mall and lock a middle-aged woman in his welling gaze. As she poured out her hard times I realized that all the clichés of American politics become real in the passion to touch and be touched. I needed to see Obama play on the field of ritual connection.

I chose Laconia, a small city in New Hampshire. Hillary had been here earlier, and she would soon be back with Bill in tow. But today, it was Obama's turn, and, in the sunshine about four hundred people had gathered in a park overlooking the nation's oldest unaltered textile mill, recently converted into a tourist center and gift shop. (What *hasn't* been refurbished for tourism in these parts?) The crowd, as far as I could tell, was uniformly white.

The people of New Hampshire are not known for adulation, and they are used to being courted by candidates on a quadrennial basis. So there were no screams, just courteous applause when Obama came bounding out of the mill in a white open-collar shirt and dark khaki slacks. He stopped to kiss a blond baby. "Who made this beautiful weather?" he exclaimed, opening his arms. "The man upstairs, huh?"

His speech was similar to the one I had seen him deliver at the United Church of Christ synod, right down to his favorite bash-the-media quip: "Some reporters call me a hope monger, a hope peddler. But I know that's what people are looking for." The crowd sensed an applause line—but they didn't clap. "I've been trying to find out what you stand for," said a woman who gave her age as eighty-five, "and I'd be very glad to know." He replied, "You look great for eighty-five."

In the field, Bill Clinton bore into people, riveting them on his big pink bozo frame. Obama doesn't hug (come to think of it, that might be a problem for a black man); he shakes hands. He doesn't burn; he simmers. He doesn't offer any fire-up refrains; he runs on an even blue flame. But his years as a community organizer show in his ability to seem like he is listening even when he's talking.

This presentation was aimed at the crowd that had come to see him. There was a pitch on affordable student loans (the House was about to pass a bill phasing out the $18 billion subsidy to lenders and offering the loans directly, at a lower interest rate), a promise to push for a federal Human Rights Act that "applies to sexual orientation" (New Hampshire had just passed a civil-union law), and finally a statement most Democrats will make only in progressive precincts, the one he couldn't quite get out when he was asked what he would do if American cities were attacked: "The threat that we face now is nowhere near as dire as it was in the Cold War. We shouldn't allow our politics to be driven simply by the fear of terrorism."

No one demanded to know why this civil libertarian voted to renew the USA PATRIOT Act, or why this advocate for human rights won't support same-sex marriage, or what this friend of the middle-class means when he says that, when it comes to Social Security, "everything should be on the table." New Englanders are famous for their skepticism, but Obama's style disarmed that reflex. It would have burst the feel-good bubble, and the most salient thing about watching him speak to white people is that he makes them feel very good.

As the sedative effect of his remarks set in, I began to wonder about this contentment. Then something occurred to me. I had stopped noticing the thing that is always on my mind when I think of Obama. I forgot about his race. And it was a very pleasant feeling, this interlude when I could look at a black man and not see, before anything else, his skin. From the happy faces around me, I deduced that other white people were enjoying the same suspension of awareness. I mean the knowledge that you notice black folks in a special way; the aching evidence that you share the perceptions of your ancestors and that you haven't completely outgrown your childhood. I am old enough to remember when it was permissible for a white man with a coaled-up face and sour-cream lips to appear on television as an entertainer. (That minstrel charade lasted into the '60s.) On some level, the image still obtrudes when I encounter a black stranger. I know it must, because I wince, as if to keep it down. Perhaps that is the key to Obama's appeal for people like me: He brings relief. A sense that, for a few moments, you have overcome. And it feels so . . . light.

What is it worth, this fleeting sensation? Is it another spell that hides the machinery of power? Another image of change that masks more of the same? Or are these feelings a harbinger of what might actually happen if the knot of race is truly untied? All sorts of other knots will open; all sorts of possibilities will be explored. We will dare again. That is what the vision of transracialism promises—and that may be the meaning of Barack Obama. For his is a dream politics, and dreams have a way of coming forth, if not coming true.

But now the happy hour is over. He must leave for a private meeting with local Democratic officials, including the head of his campaign in New Hampshire (who happens to be a lobbyist). He pauses in retreat to let the crowd surround him. The secret service prods him gently along. But a tow-headed tyke in a Superman cape intercedes. He holds out his little pink hand. Obama stoops to shake it. America the Beautiful. Cameras snap.

—*In memory of Ellen Willis*

Al Gore's Big Idea

DEAN KUIPERS

Global warming is the perfect issue for Washington to hype for the next election, and then ignore, which is why Al Gore probably won't be your next president.

By the time Al Gore appeared on *Good Morning America* in May 2007, it felt like American journalism had decided to take him down a peg, to punish him for trying to run an experiment in mass enlightenment, or to run without running, instead of joining the braying donkey race. It just didn't make sense that an ex–vice president who was so clearly campaigning and so wildly popular— who starred in a movie that won an Oscar, who was being considered for a Nobel Peace Prize, and whose environmental crusade had made him a household name to people who'd forgotten he'd almost been president— would also challenge the idea that partisan victory was the only thing that mattered.

Major news outlets gently chided him, with *Time*, the *New York Times Magazine*, the *Los Angeles Times*, and others running major features in May around the release of his new book, *The Assault on Reason*, but only with billboard headlines that hammered at their true obsession:

"Will he run?" The subtext of every interview was: *You can't be Superman* and *Clark Kent. You have to choose the realm above or the realm below.* They were ready to make him king, but only if he rolled in pig shit first, like everybody else.

And so it wasn't only *Good Morning America*'s Diane Sawyer whom Gore was scolding when she tried to ignore the critical content of his book, peppering him instead with wearying attempts to get him to say something about the 2008 race. Even as Gore protested this was "not a political book," but about "how can we reinvigorate the role of we, the people, in American democracy . . . so that those in both parties who are supposed to be making these decisions [regarding Iraq or the climate crisis] . . . are looking at the facts, and not brushing past them," Sawyer interrupted him a half-dozen times, finally saying:

"I want to get deeper into your thesis, but again, to get back to something not very deep: Donna Brazile, your former campaign manager, says, 'If he loses twenty-five to thirty pounds, that means he's running.' Have you lost any weight?"

"Listen to your questions!" Gore pleaded. "The horserace, the cosmetic parts of this—while we're focused on Britney and K-Fed and Anna Nicole Smith and all this stuff . . . our country has made some very serious mistakes that could be avoided if we, the people, including the news media, are involved in an informed and vigorous discussion of what our choices are."

Gore is right. American democracy is ill. When I looked at my feet, I noticed I had my pig-barn boots on, too. Who could blame him for skipping the campaign's withering diminution? Or even for believing he can be more effective by staying out of Washington altogether?

Days after the Sawyer interview, he laid out his current platform most succinctly on NPR's *All Things Considered*: "I'm involved in a different kind of campaign myself—to make sure that the climate crisis is the number one issue on the agenda of candidates in both parties. And I know that sounds like an unrealistic goal right now, but I will wager that by the time the elections of November 2008 come around, it will be the number one issue in both parties."

And yes, maybe the only way to make sure that happens is to run for president, and Gore was very careful to leave the door open a crack. Measuring that crack has great entertainment value: In November 2006, Vegas was giving odds of 1000 to 1 against a Gore candidacy (bet you wished now you'd locked in a grand back then), but by Summer 2007 they had slimmed to 4 to 1, running only behind Obama (7-2) and Hillary Clinton (8-5). And so the paradox: as long as he keeps teasing us, he remains most effective both as a Democratic contender and as a global warming crusader, sucking the media along in his wake. Yet he tells the people in his Alliance for Climate Protection, who are working like devils to make the climate crisis the top issue, that he's not running. He told this to the armies of people who put together Live Earth, the hulking—if lackluster—July 7 concerts that had hoped to take his message to 2 billion people. He tells it to his wife and kids.

But leaving the door open a crack is, in this case, evidence of a man in deep conflict. Not only about the efficacy of being president as it concerns global warming, but about the office itself. He was already in the White House for eight years, remember, and failed utterly to make anyone in Washington care about global warming, even for a minute. The details create a rich metaphor for Washington as a place where big ideas go to die: Gore has been engaged in the climate change issue for over thirty years, and even made it a big plank in his own 1988 run for the Democratic presidential nomination, but that kind of realism hit a brick wall within the halls of power. In a May 21, 2007 piece in the *New York Times Magazine,* Gore refused to blame this on his boss, Bill Clinton, but his responses make it clear he was shocked by how much the presidency is compromised. During the 1997 negotiations on the Kyoto Protocol on climate change, nearly every advisor close to the administration told Gore not even to attend the meetings, but he did anyway, and came back with a treaty for Clinton to sign. Bubba did sign it, but was so sure the Senate would not ratify it that he never even sent it over there.

That's where America's official position on climate change has sat ever since. Perhaps it's different now. Perhaps there's the political will to ratify such a treaty after the 2006 mid-terms, and only the Executive Branch stands in the way. But industry wields enormous power. Perhaps the truly depressing message of his I'm-not-running mantra is that it wields too much power.

So Gore has decided to mainline the issue straight to the public in great populist broadsides. After Live Earth, one can feel that effort faltering. And if he doesn't run, the press will eventually shine the spotlight somewhere else. The circus moves on. But that doesn't mean climate change falls off the agenda. In fact, he may have achieved his goal already, whipping the issue into a juggernaut that is just too politically expedient to ignore, cutting a swath toward the next election on a wave of green feel-good. Everyone assumed that he was using the issue to run for president. What if he was just using a run for president to push the issue? It's hard not to feel pimped, especially after eight years of Bush, but it's also remarkably refreshing. Senators make crap presidential candidates because of their maddening practice of manufacturing non-answers for every question. Gore has staked his entire political life on one clear answer to what he considers to be The Most Important Issue.

As the articulation of that issue, Gore's book and movie, *An Inconvenient Truth*, have had spectacular moments of influence. In April 2007, George W. Bush's very own US Supreme Court ruled that carbon dioxide and other so-called global warming gasses could be considered pollutants and could, thus, be regulated by the US Environmental Protection Agency. Not that they had to be, but that they could be.

Before *An Inconvenient Truth*, that decision probably would have gone the other way. Gore isn't inventing this new environmental consciousness—the vindictive removals of several anti-environmental incumbents during the 2006 elections made it clear that a lot of Americans are ready for that—but he has helped flip the advantage from doubters to believers, stockpiling political and cultural capital and giving millions of Americans a single locus for all their discontent with corporate politics as it exists now—and a clear way to change it.

"Back in 1982, Al said to me that he thought the environment would become the single most important organizing principle of the twenty-first century. Now, we're darn near close to that," said Rick Jacobs, the former California chair of the 2004 Howard Dean campaign who's worked with Gore in campaigns and in the corporate world. "I don't think that Al Gore thinks that this is a partisan issue, not for one minute. This is not about ideology, this is not about borders, this is not about one person benefiting and another person not benefiting. It's not a zero-sum game.

"Does he end up using that? I don't think [he] has to," he added. "With the concerts all over the world this summer, the involvement of corporations and individuals, and the kind of hip nature of environmental support—I mean, it's really become *the big thing*—he doesn't have to run for president. I think that what he does with this, it sounds really corny, but I think he saves the planet."

Before Gore's movie, there were only cursory attempts to launch legislation addressing climate change, but now, little more than a year later, steam is building on Capitol Hill for a knock-down, drag-out fight over this issue, and possibly as soon as Fall 2007. With Democrats controlling key committee positions, the two top bills—Henry Waxman's Safe Climate Act in the House, and the Barbara Boxer–Bernie Sanders Global Warming Pollution Reduction Act in the Senate—are rolling up sponsors.

Still, one only needs look at the dirty fight being waged by the EPA to see how easily Washington can turn aside Gore's big idea.

Boxer has called a series of hearings in which she has excoriated Bush's EPA chief, Stephen Johnson, for actively resisting the implementation of a California law that would set toughest-in-the-nation limits on greenhouse gas tailpipe emissions for cars and light trucks. The EPA needs to issue a waiver in order to give California the go-ahead, and though Johnson has promised to make a decision by the end of 2007, Boxer pointed out that his meetings with key polluters like the automobile industry have indicated he will not grant the waiver—the first denial among the forty-odd waiver requests California has made since the federal Clean Air Act was amended in 1970.

Fran Pavley introduced and passed those emissions limits in 2002, when she was in the California Assembly. They would cut carbon emissions by 74 million metric tons per year by 2020, and go a long way toward meeting overall carbon reduction targets. Now running for the state Senate, Pavley, too, has been dogging Stephen Johnson, pressing him for that waiver. Because of its historic problems with smog, the Clean Air Act has a little hitch written into it that allows California to set air quality standards more stringent than the feds. Other states then have the option to choose between California or federal regulations.

Much to the displeasure of the car companies, twelve other states have chosen California's new standards. Their requirements are not measured in miles per gallon, but they would mean that cars and trucks would need to get about 43 MPG to be road legal. The EPA argued that it wasn't even allowed to rule on this issue, as it didn't regulate greenhouse gases, which is the question the Supreme Court settled in April.

So now the whole country is waiting for Johnson to make a decision that will affect roughly half the drivers in the nation, and it's all on him and his boss, George W. Bush. California? Those people can go to hell. No matter what the people want, the EPA can tell them no.

"Governor Schwarzenegger asked me to accompany him to a meeting with Stephen Johnson, to ask him in person," says Pavley, who made the trip to Washington in May. "The governor tried to push him on a timeline for making a decision on the waiver. It's handled administratively. It doesn't have to go through Congress, any of that. And Stephen Johnson stalled, even in his comments. He said, 'Well, it's a very complex issue. We're not sure how it overlaps with the federal Corporate Average Fuel Economy, or CAFE standards.' Then he brought up the lawsuits [in which the auto industry is suing three of the states], which should be irrelevant to a waiver process. And I came away with the direct impression that he must be under a lot of pressure from—I'm just guessing on this—from the West Wing or political powers to delay this.

"The governor said, 'Well, providing we can meet the waiver test and all that, are you generally supportive of what we're trying to do here?'

He said he wasn't prepared to answer that question. "Privately, there are people in EPA who have told me that they think this is an absolutely important measure, because mobile sources are such an important contributing factor to greenhouse gas emissions. And essentially, without saying it directly, they're saying this is going to be a political decision."

★ ★ ★

Gore's big rock festival, Live Earth, almost went this way, too: the original plan called for a giant concert on the National Mall in Washington, DC, a huge, non-partisan love fest . . . until the Republican leadership in the Senate killed it.

"That's why Live Earth came about: If governments aren't going to act, we need to act," said John Rego about a month before the Live Earth shows. Rego was in charge of greening the Live Earth experience, along with John Picard, a former member of President Clinton's Green White House Task Force.

Only the day before Live Earth actually happened, a smaller Washington DC concert was added, but it was hardly the grand and patriotic affair that had been intended. When Live Earth's original application to use the mall was denied (the space was double-booked, said the National Park Service), Senate Majority Leader Harry Reid, a Democrat, and Senator Olympia Snowe, a Republican, drafted a bi-partisan resolution to stage the concert on the steps of the US Capitol Building instead, which faces the mall.

"A small number of senators used parliamentary maneuverings to block it. Chief among them was Senator Inhofe, Republican from Oklahoma. He is Washington's denier-in-chief, when it comes to global warming," said Live Earth Communications Director Yusef Robb. Inhofe's published reasoning was that it was a "partisan political event." Senate Minority Leader Mitch McConnell and others were also against the measure.

James Inhofe had been in the room when Gore testified about global warming before Congress in March, and didn't like what he heard. Admittedly, Gore was swinging for the fence. He advocated an immediate freeze on CO_2 emissions in the US and reducing those levels 90 percent by 2050. (Just for comparison, Bush finally confronted the issue at the G-8 summit in early June and proposed reductions of, ahem, 0 percent.) One way to do it, Gore said, was to kill the payroll tax and impose a "carbon tax," thus embedding the cost of pollution (we can say that now—thanks Supreme Court!) in the market. He wants greatly increased gas mileage on cars and a moratorium on new coal-fired power plants except those that can sequester their carbon. In order to get industry on board, he's advocating a cap-and-trade system that would allow heavy greenhouse gassers like coal companies to buy "credits" from, say, solar producers, thus offsetting the carbon by increasing profits and investment in clean industries, producing a "carbon neutral" result.

Inhofe was right to be alarmed. Little more than a year before, he could have given this talk a Bush-like brush-off, saying global warming wasn't proven and had little to do with government policy. But in March, he was like the last dinosaur looking for a place to lie down. Several major polls released in the spring revealed that three-quarters of Americans believed global warming was a serious problem and a large majority believed it was related to human activity that needed to be addressed.

And if that wasn't enough, Gore's movie had twisted most of Hollywood into a kind of panic over the issue.

Even the décor of the Beverly Hills offices of Control Room, the production company that put on Live Earth, conveyed a sense of crisis, with big countdown clocks on the wall and hurriedly hired staff working in shifts and piling on the frequent flier miles. The sense of mission was palpable and half the town—from celebs like Cameron Diaz and Leonardo DiCaprio, to Mayor Antonio Villaraigosa and the Los Angeles City Council, to do-gooder production types—got swept up in it.

"The key to all of this is: how do you tie music to a message? If you can tie the two, you get an emotional transfer," said Kevin Wall, owner of Control Room and the producer of Live Earth. He would know, having produced more than three hundred events by artists like Bob Dylan, but also Amnesty International concerts, the Freddie Mercury Tribute Concert for AIDS Awareness at Wembley Stadium in London, and the eight-concert Live 8 event, which was meant to force the G-8 countries to confront global poverty. Live 8 brought in pledges of tens of billions of dollars from the world's economic superpowers, and at the time of this writing it wasn't known how much Live Earth brought in for Gore's Alliance for Climate Protection, but Wall says these shows do more than just raise money.

"In the late 1980s, the apartheid issue was not a well-known problem outside South Africa," said Wall, describing an album project he was involved in with Springsteen guitarist (and future Soprano), Steven Van Zandt, called *Sun City: Artists United Against Apartheid*. "That resulted in a massive event at Wembley Stadium called the 'Free Nelson Mandela Show.' That show was in seventy-one countries. That project took the apartheid issue to the globe and allowed people to say, 'Oh, I won't buy from companies that do business there.' Six months later—within *six months!*—a guy whose picture had not been seen for twenty-five years (no one had a [recent] picture of Nelson Mandela, he was in Robben Island) was let out of prison.

"And so all those years of great work in South Africa, when tied globally to music and transferring that emotion, there was a change."

The fact that nations and municipalities rushed to be included in the Live Earth event may be evidence that, after decades of groundwork, such change is imminent on the global warming front. Wall and his staff limited the concerts to nine—at Giants Stadium in New York; Wembley Stadium in London; Aussie Stadium in Sydney; Copacabana Beach in Rio de Janeiro; Maropeng at the Cradle of Humankind in Johannesburg; Makuhari Messe in Tokyo; the Steps of the Oriental Pearl Tower in Shanghai; HSH Nordbank Arena in Hamburg; and Washington DC (Inonu Stadium in Istanbul was cancelled)—to run consecutively over a twenty-four hour period. But they fielded requests from L.A. to Ulan Bator for ways to be involved, and the shows were viewed at over two hundred other public screenings worldwide.

Wall and his staff also engineered one of the biggest dog-piles of what's politely called "media penetration" in history: In the US alone, the show was on NBC prime time for three hours; several cable networks for twenty-four hours; both satellite radio networks, on several channels, for twenty-four hours; thousands of radio stations; MSN broadband; and a wireless carrier. Then, there are the other one hundred countries. In the UK, they got BBC1 and the company let them rebuild a master control studio to handle the feeds. In Japan they had both NHK and Fuji-TV, first-time-ever cooperation between commercial and non-commercial stations there. Plus a universe of satellite and Internet overlays. A lot of it was captured in HD. The plans, anyway, were massive.

In the end, it turned out that regular TV-watching folks weren't that turned on by the idea of another benefit concert, and in many markets Live Earth was third or fourth in the local ratings. It did less well than the 2005 broadcasts of Live 8 in most places. It did better online, and is being touted as the most-watched webcast event ever. But it was even criticized by Live Aid founder Sir Bob Geldoff and The Who's Roger Daltrey as not having much connection to the issue.

Still, smack at the focal point of those tens of millions of eyeballs and a campaign strategist's wet dream of earned media, was Al Gore, making the logical extension of his humble slideshow that was the inspiration for *An Inconvenient Truth*. It might not have been the grand slam he'd wanted, but the stated strategy of Gore and his activist organization, Alliance for Climate Protection, is to keep the issue in the public eye. Wall says this message of global climate emergency is the "ask."

"This project is a launch event for a several-year campaign that will continue to make movement at the level of governments, the level of corporations, and the level of consumers. But this [is] a very aggressive, very deep, and very big ask as a beginning," Wall said.

You know that an issue has really moved Hollywood when it inspires them to talk about their children. Director James Cameron was standing at a podium, speaking to director Davis Guggenheim and Al Gore about their film, *An Inconvenient Truth*.

"In spite of being a colossal downer, it manages to convey hope," he said, as he presented the pair with the 2007 Santa Barbara Film Festival David Attenborough Award for excellence in nature filmmaking. The maker of *Titanic* and *The Terminator* was the 2006 winner of this award, for his 3-D IMAX film, *Ghosts of the Abyss*, but, like many in Hollywood, is not known for any particularly pointed political message in his work beyond straightforward conservation, nor any particular romance with political campaigning.

Gore evidently changed the way he feels about these matters, however. After a few laudatory sentences about the movie, he suddenly turned to Gore, and all 2,000 people in the auditorium seem to be urging him on as he said, "The global crisis presented in this film calls for a change in leadership. We need a true leader for the twenty-first century. I think you can see where I'm going with this, and we'll probably have words about it later"—Gore gave him a sidelong glance, shaking his head—"but I beseech you, for the sake of our children, to step up to the plate one more time and run for president."

Gore sat, acknowledging the thunderous standing ovation that immediately erupted and the chant that has greeted Gore at nearly every public event for the last year—"Run, Al, Run!" He pointed his finger briefly at Cameron, mouthing "I owe you one."

I have seen Gore at four or five Hollywood occasions and some version of this scene is repeated everywhere he goes.

I was in Lawrence Bender's back yard in the Holmby Hills section of L.A. with some people from the Rainforest Action Network in May, thinking about that "ask." Bender, the producer of *An Inconvenient Truth*, as well as most of Quentin Tarantino's films, has been moved by his exposure to Gore and the science to launch a campaign called 18 Seconds (18seconds.org)—the amount of time it takes to change out one light bulb for an energy-saving compact fluorescent.

Looking at his posh digs and guests—there was Darryl Hannah, Tom Hayden, actor (and Charlize Theron's boyfriend) Stuart Townsend, Fran Pavley, a host of rich neighbors signing checks—one bulb almost seemed like a joke. In fact, many scientists and even the heads of many environmental groups who want more radical action on global warming have said the same: changing one bulb doesn't do shit for helping global warming. But maybe that's too hasty. This is where we misunderstand Al Gore, too: these people are not going to solve our problems with one sweeping gesture or one monster piece of legislation.

Instead, they are changing corporate and governmental behavior by changing cultural behavior. Wal-Mart and Yahoo got involved in Bender's campaign, and by mid-2007 they'd moved 55,434,116 bulbs, preventing over 24 billion pounds of CO_2 emissions in six months.

"Let's get people to do one thing. And once you do one thing, you're going to feel good, and you're going to say, what else can I do?" said Bender. He thinks of the compact fluorescent light bulb as a Trojan horse, embedding the "ask." Hollywood is particularly good at that kind of thing—and Gore spends a lot of time in L.A. His screen-writer daughter Kristin Gore Cusack lives there. Seriously, anybody who's ever been in a room with Al Gore long enough to wonder how we all missed the fact that he's charismatic comes out with a global warming strategy. Cameron Diaz drives her Prius and flies carbon neutral.

Salma Hayek and Jake Gyllenhaal went to the Arctic to check out the receding ice. Leo DiCaprio has produced a feature-length documentary about the climate crisis, *The 11th Hour*, which is being hailed as this year's big eco-doc; Brad Pitt's doing spots about how New Orleans needs to be protected from the future effects of climate change. At this year's Oscars, Gore and a dozen other stars rolled up to the red carpet in alternative-fueled cars instead of limos—some of which were organized by a branch of former Russian president Mikhail Gorbachev's eco-organization, Global Green USA.

"Everyone is asking—stockholders are asking their CEOs—what are you doing about this issue? And most major global and national companies are getting asked: what are you doing? People are asking their legislators," Bender added.

Organizers hoped that Live Earth would expose about one-third of the people on planet Earth to a series of simple messages—a kind of at-home, board game version of the big show Gore laid out to Congress in March. The final numbers on Live Earth weren't that big, but at the very least the concerts themselves were used as demonstration projects for the ways that the entertainment industry could change its carbon-hogging behavior.

"The venue that puts a smile on my face is Johannesburg," said Rego, whose background is in advising private industry on these matters. "The first call to the Johannesburg promoter, he said, 'Look: I have no idea what greening means'—he understands, but not what it really means in terms of an event—and he says, 'but I'm willing to learn, and I'm really excited about it.'"

Unlike Wembley, which is in London and has thus been

catering to carbon-phobic pop stars for years, the Johannesburg site didn't even actually exist. Maropeng at the Cradle of Humankind is a big grassy field about 50-60 kilometers outside Jo'burg with no stage and few facilities other than a nearby convention hall. This venue is one where buying power exclusively from renewable sources would be double or triple the normal price, and thus be impossible for a local promoter to replicate in the future, which is a vital part of the Live Earth program. So they used biodiesel generators and bought carbon offsets—the DIY version of cap-and-trade, in which energy users from bands to businessmen pay a kind of indulgence which is invested in eco-friendly projects like turning cow manure into fuel. Vendors were connected to suppliers of biodegradable corn plastics and composting and recycling. Lighting onstage, in trailers, and in studios were all LED or compact fluorescents, and even hotels hosting Live Earth artists were being encouraged to swap out for eco-friendly bulbs; signage was made from recycled or agricultural materials. Most of the much-criticized air travel by Live Earth staff and artists was offset by carbon credits.

The US Green Building Council, creators of the LEED green building rating system, helped Rego and others collate best practices into a new set of Green Event Guidelines, which they hope will transform the entertainment industry.

In Sydney, for example, the city created an integrated concert ticket that included free transit to and from Aussie Stadium. (L.A.'s Hollywood Bowl has had this program for some time, and Live Earth is hoping it will spread.) Hamburg similarly embedded .30 Euros in each ticket for carbon offsets. Rio appointed a special city

commissioner to help with the concert, and the big tri-
umph there was to connect the gargantuan waste stream
with the traditional community of poor residents who
make their money off the city's robust plastic and alu-
minum recycling programs.

The one hundred or so bands who played Live Earth
received an eighty to ninety-page binder talking all about
everything from biodiesel tour buses to carbon offsets to
writing up a tour "eco-rider"—an environmental version
of the document that tells promoters what kinds of food
and amenities they require. Bands are already ahead of the
curve on this, with acts like the Dave Matthews band traveling bio-diesel and carbon neutral since 2001, and green
tour marketing companies like MusicMatters reporting a
huge recent jump in clients. For many cities, this smells like
money; Hamburg's mayor saw Live Earth as the perfect
opportunity to sell his town to the green tech industry. Privately, many of the Live Earth venues confided to Rego
that "they know their venue is the greenest."

Which brings us back to Al Gore. He is, if you haven't
noticed, a very successful capitalist and a gadget nut, and
has been a leading proponent of using the market to
address the climate crisis. That has led to a few embarrassing revelations—like the news that the Gore mansion
in Nashville gobbled up 221,000 kilowatt-hours of juice
in 2006, about twenty times more than the nation's average home—but it turns out that Gore can buy offsets for
that from his own company, having founded Generation
Investment Management LLP in 2004. It's a standard
investment firm and hedge fund, co-founded with David
Blood, former chief executive of Goldman Sachs Asset
Management (hence the cutesy nickname "Blood and

Gore"), which is "dedicated to long-term investing, integrated sustainability research, and client alignment." That's Wall-Street-ese for: "boatloads of money from the hot green market."

Does the old world end, then, not with a bang or a whimper, but with a "ka-ching?" This market-driven approach to change has also been roundly criticized as an inherently limited strategy. But, at the very least, Live Earth viewers were saturated with messages conveying simple solutions they can put into effect right now, like:

RIDE A BIKE

BANK ONLINE

SAY NO TO STYROFOAM

UPGRADE YOUR PC [Instead of buying a new one]

GROW TOMATOES

You can bet the Democratic National Committee would absolutely love to add one more, saying:

VOTE DEMOCRAT

Or even:

ELECT AL GORE

But that, said Kevin Wall, was not part of the messaging. "What can I tell you? I think he'd make a great president," said Wall. "But I have to go with what he tells me, and he tells me he's not running."

☆　☆　☆

Red carpet interview by Dean Kuipers at the Santa Barbara International Film Festival with former ER *star Noah Wyle and his wife, Tracy Warbin.*

NOAH WYLE: I look at the success of [*An Inconvenient Truth*] as a testament to his leadership ability. The fact that he was able to go outside the beltway completely, and find a way and a medium to communicate directly with people on an issue as significant as this—and he came across as personable and as intelligent as he did—

TRACY WARBIN: and he's already won once, as well. He knows how to do it.

NOAH WYLE: I think more people have seen this movie than were able to see him in any of those [2000] debates, and I think that his persona came across mostly through the caricatures that people made of him, rather than him putting himself forward with his beliefs and the passion with which he espouses those beliefs. It comes through very strongly in this film. And I think, hopefully, it's a new form of campaigning.

New Mexico governor Bill Richardson *is* running for president, however, and if you have any question about the viable environmental space Gore and the Iraq War have lent Campaign 2008, you might start with the "man-on-the-moon" energy and climate planks in Richardson's presidential platform. When he announced his candidacy in the chandeliered Gold Room at Los Angeles's Biltmore Hotel—the same room in which John F. Kennedy accepted the 1960 Democratic nomination for president—he compared his climate protection initiative to the Apollo program, saying, "When John F. Kennedy challenged this

AI Gore

country to reach the moon, he challenged us to get there
in ten years, not twenty or thirty or forty." He proudly
identified his green policy to be the most aggressive of any
candidate—with John Edwards and Chris Dodd close seconds—saying, "we need it much faster and more boldly
than people are suggesting."

People like who, Bush? The guy who went to the G-8
summit trying desperately to kill any notion of binding
carbon emissions limits, which Germany's Angela Merkel
had put at the top of the agenda? That's too easy. No, he
means just about *all* other people—except Gore. And the
fact that Richardson would step out like this shows how
much the issue has changed since he was Energy Secretary
in the Clinton-Gore administration, and saw the vice president struggle and fail to get Kyoto on the agenda.

The UN-affiliated Intergovernmental Panel on Climate
Change, whose gold-plated science Gore (and everyone
else) cites constantly, recommends an 80 percent reduction in greenhouse gas emissions by 2050 in order to hold
global warming to two degrees Celsius. The top House
and Senate bills both go for 80 percent. Gore says 90 percent. Richardson says 90 percent, too.

"Yeah, I talked to him," Richardson said off-stage,
referring to Gore. "In fact, the day I announced them. We
talked briefly on the phone, and I believe he liked it."

Richardson's plan also reflects the newest iteration of
this issue among scientists, pols, and activists: energy policy and climate change policy are now the same thing.

"It's bigger than Iraq. It's about national security,
period," said Tony Massaro, senior vice president for Political Affairs and Public Education at the League of
Conservation Voters. "Our polling on Election Night 2006,

by a prominent Republican pollster, Frank Luntz, showed that when people were thinking about national security, they were thinking about our energy policy."

Since that election, Massaro said, Gore's movie helped fuse energy policy and global warming policy into one issue, and the league is tracking 2008 presidential candidates' responses to that issue with their initiative, "The Heat is On" (http://www.heatison.org), which includes a handy comparison chart. Massaro pointed out the sea change attending that chart, saying, "The most important thing is that those numbers have been driven not by the vice president but by what the science has said is needed." Science, he said, creates the space for audacious plans like Richardson's, and the beauty is that any enlightened Republican or Independent candidate could do the same.

They haven't yet, however, suggesting that Republicans are determined, like Inhofe and McConnell, to make this a partisan issue. Already in May, eighteen months before the election, at least six of the Democratic candidates had detailed their energy and climate plans before taking published policy positions on healthcare, taxes, Iraq, or other key issues. Hillary Clinton, Barack Obama, Chris Dodd, and Joe Biden are backing the Sanders-Boxer bill for 80 percent reduction by 2050, and Dennis Kucinich supports the Waxman bill. On the Republican side, McCain has sponsored a bill that calls for a 65 percent reduction by 2050, but he's the only one who has articulated reduction targets. Several other Republicans, such as Sam Brownback, are on record as having opposed carbon reduction bills and a cap-and-trade system.

Richardson's plan also calls for getting out of a Middle-Eastern quagmire by cutting oil demand by 50 percent by

2020. That's only thirteen years from now, by which time he wants cars to get 50 mpg (as compared to John Edward's 40 mpg, or Bush's 35 mpg). By 2020, he would also set standards to reduce the carbon impact of all liquid fuels by 30 percent and require electrical generation to have a 30 percent renewable portfolio standard—an achievable goal, given that twenty-one states have already adopted robust RPS criteria, but still ten percent higher than anyone else is proposing.

All this talk would seem as inflated as mid-1990s thinking about dot-coms—except that the energy sector is already there.

Jim Rogers, CEO of Duke Energy, a carbon-belching electric utility headquartered deep in the heart of West Virginia's coal country, has emerged as a leading advocate of a cap-and-trade system for emissions and has challenged Bush and Cheney on their foot-dragging. Big Power evidently agrees, because they selected Rogers to chair the Edison Electric Institute, which represents about 60 percent of the electricity generated in this country, and have begun lumbering toward climate-change goals.

And power companies aren't the only ones seeing the (compact fluorescent) light: Rogers helped start the US Climate Action Partnership, a coalition of serious environmental groups like the NRDC and industrial and financial giants including DuPont, Duke, Caterpillar, Alcoa, and PG&E, some of which are among the world's largest single carbon emitters—whose purpose is to pressure the Bush administration into building these carbon reduction costs into the market. Pepsi and GM are recent joiners, and not just because it's the right thing to do; *it pays*. The visionary Chicago Climate Exchange has already begun to institutionalize emissions and carbon futures trading: though the system is voluntary and still young, leaders in the Climate Action Partnership foresee an emissions market worth $750 billion—yes, with a "b"—within twenty years. That kind of money could power an investment super-boom in clean technologies.

All of which is a sad commentary on the fear and stasis gripping Washington. Obama, for instance, has hedged his bets by backing the Sanders-Boxer bill *and* co-sponsoring an ugly bill that is a gift to the coal industry, locking the US into a long-term program of deep subsidies and guaranteed purchases of heavily polluting coal-to-liquid fuels. The climate protection armies are betting he can't maintain that position if pushed by the grassroots, and Gore doesn't have to run to make sure that happens. It's happening now.

"People are getting it," said Lawrence Bender, who has spoken on the subject to the Conference of Mayors and in the California Assembly. "As an agent I'm very close to said to me, 'Lawrence, I'm a Republican. My kids need to live in the same world your kids live in.' It cannot be a one-sided issue, or the problems will never be solved. It's too small of thinking."

"One of these folks (or someone not yet in the race) is going to be president. Maybe after they lose, the others can take a leaf from Al Gore and Bill Bradley and get serious about how to fix the country."
—Jonathan Alter, *Newsweek*, June 18, 2007

In late spring, I was at a little gathering of enviro types in Venice, California and one of them explained while networking fiercely that his project was to get top artists to write 1,000 songs about global warming by 2008. Melissa Etheridge had done pretty well with this idea, winning an Oscar for the song she wrote for *An Inconvenient Truth*, "I Need to Wake Up." My reaction was: what an absolutely terrible idea. If I were a seventeen-year-old kid looking for the music that's going to define my age, and instead was hearing even three or four syrupy pop hits about global warming all at any one time, I'd immediately launch a pro-coal anti-movement, call myself the Carbonators or the Tar Sands or something, just to bring the fun back.

But, alas, look for a lot of messaging about the climate flying around MySpace in the next year, especially with folks like hip-hop megaproducer Pharell Williams of the Neptunes signed onto the campaign. Whether these efforts lead to brilliance, like Marvin Gaye's "What's Going On?" or something else altogether, like another "We are the World," Gore is out there leading the new culture war. As of this writing, Gore's new book, *The Assault on Reason*, has been lodged in lists of top five bestsellers at Amazon and on the *New York Times*. The book version of *An Inconvenient Truth* has sold 850,000 copies, with a new young adult version just arriving and a children's version on the way. The slide show is being translated into twenty-eight languages, and over 1,200 people have gone through training at Gore's Nashville offices to deliver spin-off version of the show, with new presenters to be trained in China and India soon.

Could a reality show be far behind? Will ordinary people be lining up in malls around the country to audition for *Save the Planet*, or some such?

If that's what it takes, says Cathy Zoi, CEO of Gore's Alliance for Climate Protection, to actually change behavior. Live Earth's low ratings might indicate that people are already hip to global warming, but Zoi says that hasn't affected our habits much.

Americans can buy tankless waterheaters and 90-percent-efficient furnaces and hybrid cars, but most of them don't—despite the fact that these items really do pay for themselves, and quickly, too. They could install solar panels or vote for mass transit instead of more highways or only eat local food. But they don't. Institutionally, Wal-Mart has made great strides by using only biodegradable corn-based plastics in their packaging, but whenever the consumer is given a lower-cost option—standard light bulbs are still cheaper than the 100 million compact fluorescents Wal-Mart's trying to sell, for example—we are much more likely to buy the cheaper one.

For Zoi, that reality dictates where she must direct her energies: a three-year campaign to sell climate change to the people.

"Our sweet spot is to engage in a mass communications exercise on a scale that the private sector does. So our product is persuading people that the climate crisis is both urgent and solvable. We have to reach new audiences with that message," she says.

Behold, ye footsoldiers of the carbon-neutral future, Gore and his generals are wading into the fields of the unconverted . . . to do more PR. Doesn't sound like much of a revolution, until you look at who has aligned themselves with Gore to do the selling.

Back in the early 1990s, Zoi pioneered the federal Energy Star appliance-efficiency program as a manager at the EPA and was chief of staff in the Council on Environmental Quality in the Clinton–Gore administration. Before coming to the alliance, she was group executive director at the Bayard Group in Sydney, a global for-profit company selling smart metering systems (gas and electric meters that feedback constantly to the utility, allowing more precise and higher-efficiency distribution) with $1.2 billion in revenues.

Similarly, the alliance's board of directors includes former EPA chief Carol Browner; Lehman Brothers Managing Director Theodore Roosevelt IV, who is also the chair of the Pew Center for Global Climate Change; former national security advisor to both Presidents Ford and George H. W. Bush, Brent Scowcroft; National Wildlife Federation head Larry Schweiger; and former Georgia-Pacific president Lee Thomas, among others. These are people who know how to make hay with Gore's white-hot sunlight. If executives of this kind of amperage thought the most important thing was electing a president, they'd damn well be doing that—and maybe they are. But, right now, they're also doing groundwork beyond politics.

And that, Zoi says, means the unglamorous fieldwork of evangelizing—yes, to the politicians and smart capitalists who will make it happen, but mostly to the American consumer. Evangelizing about efficient cars and appliances, cleaner electricity (no coal), removing regulatory barriers to clean energy, building large markets to drive down the cost of new technologies, designing tax breaks, creating carbon emissions markets, and so on. None of what the alliance does involves directly supporting candidates, writing legislation, or marketing products. The "ask" is the product.

"I've been doing the sustainable energy, conventional energy, electricity industry stuff for twenty years. There is no magic bullet," says Zoi. "It's probably going to be a hundred different things."

Including a whole lot more Al Gore. Even before he had finished *The Assault on Reason*, he was announcing that he would be cranking out another book moving beyond urgency to "solutions," part of which would include holding "solutions summits" with corporate, political, and scientific leaders. All this Hollywood juice—the Oscar, etc.—is driving web-savvy DIY producers to push more and more content onto Gore's Current TV media channel. That Internet channel's producers are also going after more standard youth culture programming, being the exclusive streamer of live feeds from the huge 2007 Bonnaroo festival, for example, in Gore's home state of Tennessee. Gore evidently even has a children's TV show in the works. And, of course, into May he was still doing the slideshow, sometimes twice a day when he's on a roll.

Having campaigned all his adult life, he knows this message cannot be reduced to a thirty-second campaign ad. And right there, in that one fact, might lay the whole irritating reason he cannot be president. The entire system for electing presidents is designed to exclude anything as complex as reality.

"Now, our culture has changed so much that knowledge does not play as big a role as it should in our conversations of democracy," Gore said at the 2007 Santa Barbara Film Festival, where he was in exceptionally fine form.

"If not knowledge, then what?" asked Emcee Mike DeGruy.

"Money," said Gore flatly.

Money, he went on to add, that paid for thirty-second campaign spots. He and Davis Guggenheim discussed how much more informed the voters were in the 1960s when candidates spent that money on thirty-minute campaign films about themselves and their ideas—Guggenheim's father, documentarian Charles Guggenheim, had once made one for Gore's father, Senator Al Gore, Sr.

"If you say, look, there's a crisis and it's this complicated deal and nothing in our progress is preparing us to understand because we've got quadruple the population in less than a century and we've got technologies thousands of times more powerful than our grandparents, and all of a sudden we're really screwing up the planet and we're putting 70,000 tons of global warming pollution into the atmosphere every day, changing it so dramatically, so quickly, that it's going to be devastating for our children unless we act quickly—that doesn't fit very well into a thirty-second commercial," Gore said.

Especially when all the other candidates are embracing those TV spots and saying absolutely nothing in them. Gore has been to the mountaintop and now enjoys direct communication with the American people without compromise. Don't expect him to abandon it soon.

"Unless we wake up and start fighting for it and reintroducing reason and philosophy and justice into the political discourse of this country, this is going to end. We can't let that happen," Gore said in Santa Barbara, to a standing ovation. "This is your time. You can change this right now."

The Two John Edwardses

JAMES RIDGEWAY

In the opening pages of *Four Trials*, the book on his legal cases published during the 2004 presidential primary campaign, John Edwards recalls that when he was eleven years old, he wrote an essay called "Why I Want to Be a Lawyer." He was influenced, he says, by *Perry Mason* and especially *The Fugitive*, which featured a man wrongfully accused of murder. "In my mind's eye," he says of the series' protagonist, "he is still roaming the land and still searching for justice." Edwards decided then and there that he would grow up to defend the innocent and the downtrodden.

The vignette, like so much about Edwards, is well presented and cleverly conceived. You can almost see young John, parked in front of the black-and-white TV in one of several North Carolina mill towns where he lived as a child, waiting, as he puts it, for "that final moment when wrongs would be righted." You know it's manipulative tripe, but you also believe it may contain a kernel of truth. At least, you want to believe. You want to think that the boy who would become John Edwards was truly motivated by his desire to become a crusader for justice, and not just by Perry Mason's grandstanding finales and nice suits.

Such is the predicament of many progressive voters in the 2008 presidential primary race, in which former trial

lawyer and North Carolina senator John Edwards, considered one of only three "viable" candidates for the
nomination, has positioned himself slightly to the left of
leaders Hillary Clinton and Barack Obama, especially on
questions of economic justice. Some of these voters are
hearing, in Edwards's speeches, things they have been
waiting to hear from a mainstream Democrat for twenty
years or more. At the Democratic National Committee's
winter meeting in 2007, the first major public forum for
2008 presidential candidates, "Edwards drew a rousing
reception," the *Washington Post* reported, "with a sharp
attack on Bush's plan to send more troops to Iraq and a
populist appeal for Democrats to return to their roots as
defenders of the union workers, the poor and struggling
middle-class families. 'Brothers and sisters, in times like
these, we don't need to redefine the Democratic Party,' he
said. 'We need to reclaim the Democratic Party.'"

Five weeks earlier, Edwards had announced his candidacy in the Ninth Ward of New Orleans, surrounded by
hurricane survivors who have been not only exploited by
conservatives, but also largely ignored by most liberals.
And when he stated, in that announcement, that "poverty
is the great moral issue of our time, and we all have an
obligation to do something about it," Edwards seemed
finally to be addressing what had been so conspicuously
absent from the Democratic party platform, both in the
failed 2004 presidential campaign and the triumphant
2006 mid-term elections, neither of which even paid much
lip-service to the poor. There is considerable appeal to
Edwards's decision to dedicate his campaign to ending the
"two Americas," especially when it is set against this
legacy.

Progressive voters can also find encouragement in the assessments of the mainstream press, which depict Edwards as the Southern New Democrat who left the fold of the Democratic Leadership Council to take up a populist cause. After a day on the New Hampshire campaign trail with Edwards in February, ABC's Terry Moran declared, "He's different this time around. In 2004, when he was a relative unknown, Edwards was a cheerful moderate populist. Now, in what some critics call a convenient conversion to woo liberal Democrats, Edwards is tougher, staking out positions on healthcare, national security, and the environment, much further to the left than he advocated in 2004."

Convenient or not, the idea of Edwards's "conversion" is buoyed not only by his own rhetoric but also by attacks from conservative critics. "He is a redistributionist, another word for socialist," Cal Thomas wrote in *USA Today*. "His populist jargon is nothing but class warfare, the 2007 version." Statements like these are enough to set progressive hearts beating, as are assertions that Edwards's healthcare plan is a back door to a single-payer system.

"John Edwards will give you free healthcare," William Buckley warned in the *National Review*. This is a bad thing, of course, because "everyone, in a society of allegedly free healthcare, would actually be paying the collective costs of healthcare. . . . They used to call that socialized medicine." Not to be outdone, Fox's Bill O'Reilly declared in May that Edwards had "sold his soul to far-Left interests," and also declared that "MoveOn's running him. . . . His support on the Internet is coming from the far Left, which is telling him what to do." And then there's Ann Coulter, who surely won Edwards some votes when she told her audience at the Conservative Political Action Conference, "I was going to have a few comments on the other Democratic presidential candidate, John Edwards, but it turns out that you have to go into rehab if you use the word 'faggot.'" Indeed, these comments prompted the campaign to raise "Coulter Cash," and Elizabeth Edwards to confront Coulter in a call-in on *Hardball*—where, however planned the maneuver may have been, she came off as a class act. As Barbara Ehrenreich pointed out, a more unexpected low blow came from a mainsteam media source: "Strangely, it's not Coulter, but girl-next-door Katie Couric who's hinted, in a *60 Minutes* interview with Elizabeth Edwards, that the couple might be 'capitalizing' on the disease" when they announced in March 2007 that her breast cancer, originally diagnosed and treated shortly after the 2004 election, had returned in an incurable form. Ehrenreich writes, "Can't you just see them cackling over the bone scans, eagerly calculating what the results would do for them in the polls?"

Whether it is sincere or merely shrewd—or, as is most likely the case, both—Edwards's rhetoric in defense of America's poor stands to have a much-needed and long-overdue impact on the presidential race. After accompanying Edwards on one of his many trips to New Orleans, Matt Bai wrote in the *New York Times Magazine*, "The significance of what Edwards is saying ... though, goes well beyond messaging and tactics. As the first candidate of the post-Bill Clinton, postindustrial era to lay out an ambitious antipoverty plan, he may force Democrats to contemplate difficult questions that they haven't debated in decades—starting with what they've learned about poverty since Johnson and Kennedy's time, and what, exactly, they're willing to do about it."

And yet, this same John Edwards can also come off as a snake oil salesman, a slick lawyer who has plenty of stories to tell about his legal victories defending Main Street Americans injured by uncaring or nefarious corporations and healthcare providers, but rarely mentions the fact that these multimillion dollar civil suits also made Edwards himself a very rich man. His assets total some $30 million, and while the senator likes to talk abut his days of poverty and hardship, he did not hesitate to build the largest house in North Carolina history. In between his two presidential campaigns, he worked for a hedge fund that engaged in the kinds of practices he now decries, and suggested, in an AP interview, that he had done so largely "to learn about financial markets and their relationship to poverty"— although "making money was a good thing, too." Most troubling of all is evidence that, during this same period, he used an anti-poverty foundation to fund travel, staff, consultants, and other expenses that advanced his own political career.

While conservative critics like Thomas and Buckley make absurd prognostications about Edwards turning into a new American Lenin, Bob Novak's attack cannot be shaken off so easily. "In fact, Edwards's populist rhetoric sounds about the same today as it did three years ago," Novak writes. "The big change is his performance away from the podium. Seldom has a presidential candidate undergone a trifecta like Edwards's this year—reports of the $400 haircut, a $55,000 honorarium from University of California at Davis for a speech on poverty, and the

$500,000 hedge fund salary—without his campaign imploding."

It's true that the media seems to have a double standard when it comes to Edwards, largely because of his willingness to talk about the poor. Jeff Cohen points out that "we've been shown aerial pictures of Edwards's mansion in North Carolina, but not of the mansions of the other well-off candidates," and "we've heard so much about Edwards's connection to one Wall Street firm, but relatively little about the fact that other candidates, including Democrats, are so heavily funded by Wall Street interests. . . . You see, those other pols aren't hypocrites: they don't lecture about poverty." But the facts are what they are, and it doesn't help that Edwards's campaign responds to such facts with indignant claims of unfair persecution. In June, his deputy campaign manager, Jonathan Price, sent a fundraising email headed "Haircuts and hatchet jobs," claiming that "the whole Washington establishment wants our campaign to go away: they don't want the American people to hear the message, so they attack the messenger. They call him a hypocrite because he came from nothing, built a fortune while standing up for regular people during some of their toughest times, and—heaven forbid!—he has the nerve to remember where he came from and still care passionately about guaranteeing every family the opportunities he had to get ahead."

Even in defending his candidate, Price shines a spotlight on the very contradiction—he "built a fortune while standing up for regular people during some of their toughest times"—that makes a lot of voters uncomfortable with John Edwards. In fact, "every family" cannot possibly "get ahead" the way Edwards got ahead. As a trial lawyer, and later a senator and a well-paid and well-publicized advocate, he may indeed have helped some of the poor and powerless, but in the process he also won himself enormous wealth, fame, and a political career. That's an anomaly that Edwards managed to pull off, not a model that others can emulate.

Edwards's wealth alone may not disqualify him as a defender of the poor, any more than it did Franklin Roosevelt or Bobby Kennedy, two of the wealthiest men ever to run for president. But it adds fuel to the essential question: Does Edwards present a real challenge to the system that creates such massive inequities to begin with? Is he willing to help the poor even at the expense of people in his income bracket, and the corporate entities that helped make them rich? If there were truly one America instead of two, it would be a lot harder for anyone to be as wealthy as John Edwards. The top marginal income tax rate, which stood at 39.6 percent *before* the Bush tax cuts that Edwards wants to roll back, averaged about 80 percent during FDR's presidency; in 1968, when RFK took the "poverty tours" Edwards now seeks to emulate, it was 75 percent, while corporate tax revenues as a share of the federal budget were three times what they are today.[1]

Despite believing in the sincerity of Edwards's concern for the poor, the *Times*'s Matt Bai concluded: "While he talks incessantly about economic justice, Edwards isn't proposing anything—beyond the oil company windfall tax, which Hillary Clinton has also embraced—that would strike a blow against multinational corporations or the top tier of American earners. Even in his rhetoric, Edwards seems to deliberately avoid stoking resentments or pitting one class against another the way a true populist would, unless you count taking a few easy shots at Wal-Mart."

Bai goes on to quote former Labor Secretary Robert Reich: "Rhetorically, if you're calling Edwards an economic populist, it's true he cares a lot about the poor," says Reich (who is hardly a radical, though he himself cared too much about the poor to stay for Clinton's second term). "He evinces a lot of concern for the middle class and middle-class anxieties. But he's not in any way attacking the rich or corporations. He is not explaining one fundamental fact of modern economic life, which is that the very rich have all the money."

Myths of Modern Populism

Edwards himself seems to like being called a populist. "If the word populist means that I stand with ordinary Americans against powerful interests, the answer's yes," he told *USA Today*, "but that phrase is sometimes used in an old, backward-looking way." By contrast, his populism is "very forward-looking."

That anyone like Edwards can even be called a populist shows how far the term has evolved from the iconic nineteenth-century Populist movement, which was the greatest mass democratic movement in American history. According to Lawrence Goodwyn, the pre-eminent historian of American Populism, the movement originated during the rural depression that followed the Civil War, among farmers who discovered the essential fallacy of the American work ethic and the so-called American Dream: No amount of hard work, they learned, could make up for the fact that the "laws of commerce" were stacked against them.[2] Their rebellion took place against a political landscape that had narrowed to include only two entrenched political parties. Goodwyn writes, "Everywhere—North and South, among Republicans and Democrats—business and financial entrepreneurs had achieved control of a restructured American party system." Begun as a network of local Farmers' Alliances in the South and Middle West, which formed buying and selling cooperatives to combat the system of crop loans that was turning family farmers into sharecroppers, the movement developed a broader political analysis. The movement was different from European socialism, supporting democracy and private land ownership while opposing the consolidation of power and wealth; by the 1880s its leaders were "denouncing credit merchants, railroads, trusts, money power," and the gold standard, a tool of Eastern banking interests. The same period saw early—and bloody—labor strikes, particularly the Knights of Labor's strike against the railroad baron Jay Gould. This groundswell would develop into the largest—and possibly the last—serious challenge to the concentration of power and capital in the United States.

The Populist Party won substantial blocs in the elections of 1890 and 1892, but fell apart with 1896 election, when their ideas were co-opted by the Democratic Party. Some of the populist ideas, in weakened form, were gradually worked into the overall economy—limited corporate regulation and banking reforms, an expanded concept of currency—and a few others would resurface during the New Deal. But the Populist defeat at the dawn of the twentieth century, says Goodwyn, consolidated the political system, henceforth limiting change to "reforms" that by the time of the New Deal would be decorously referred to as "liberal" or "progressive," and "reflected the shrunken vistas that remained culturally permissible." Any sort of serious challenge to our political and economic system had been laid to rest.

Oddly enough, it was Jesse Jackson, in his 1988 Democratic primary campaign, who may have come closest to reviving the original Populist spirit, and he won a surprising level of support among rural whites in places like Iowa and New Hampshire before his campaign collapsed. Otherwise, the party name has been taken over by racists like David Duke, and the term applied largely to eccentric demagogues, from Huey Long to Ross Perot. And the term "populist" in the twenty-first century apparently applies to anyone who evokes both a folksy style and any critique whatsoever of unrestrained globalization and freemarket capitalism. In the *New York Times*, for example, Robin Toner wrote in July: "On Capitol Hill and on the presidential campaign trail, Democrats are increasingly moving toward a full-throated populist critique of the current economy." In addition to John Edwards's much-discussed populist rhetoric, she cites the fact that Hillary Clinton has "increasingly focused on 'rising inequality and rising pessimism in our work force,' and suggested that another progressive era is—and ought to be—at hand."

Historically, the Progressive Era, in fact, marked the end of Populism, replacing a systemic critique with a system of reforms designed to assuage the impact of capitalism's worst excesses, while keeping the system running smoothly. But thirty years after the Reagan Revolution, when merely talking about the plight of the poor is a novelty, just such modest reforms as Edwards is proposing—raising the minimum wage, extending health insurance, supporting college tuition—may indeed sound almost radical. And John Edwards himself may be the closest thing to a populist who has a chance of making it to Super Tuesday with double-digit support.

Early Edwards

John Edwards's effort to position himself as the race's true populist—the man who understands and empathizes with the struggling masses—has gotten a leg up from his own life story. None of the Democratic frontrunners' backgrounds is particularly privileged. But while Hillary Clinton's father owned a modest textile business, Edwards's father was a floor worker in a textile mill—though he later rose to a well-paid supervisory job. Edwards was the first in his family to attend college, and his undergraduate degree from North Carolina State University, was in textile technology. Only after law school at UNC Chapel Hill—where he met and married Elizabeth Anania Edwards—did Edwards hit his stride on the path that would lead him to his current place, discovering a way to stick up for the little guy while also adding to his own personal wealth and fame.

He began his legal career with a federal clerkship and then a brief stint at a law firm in Nashville, where he defended record companies accused of pirating Elvis Presley songs. But it was when he joined a Raleigh, North Carolina firm that Edwards began to make a name for himself as a personal injury lawyer who won huge jury awards through the power of his persuasive, often emotional rhetoric. In one early case, Edwards claimed, in his closing statement, to be channeling the voice of a little girl who had suffered brain damage at birth in a botched delivery: "She speaks to you through me. And I have to tell you right now—I didn't plan to talk about this—right now I feel her. I feel her presence. She's inside me, and she's talking to you." In his most famous case, on behalf of a toddler who had been partially disemboweled by a pool drain with a defective cover, he won $25 million, the largest settlement in North Carolina history, and received a public service award from the Association of Trial Lawyers of America.

It's not clear why Edwards got into politics, or even whether he was a Democrat or Republican, before he ran for the Senate as a Democrat in 1998 against Lauch Faircloth, a hog farmer. Edwards wouldn't take money from PACs or lobbyists, and ended up spending $8.3 million— three quarters of it his own money—compared to Faircloth's $9.4 million, $1.7 million of which was his own.[3] Faircloth ran nearly a dozen negative ads targeting Edwards, most of them seeking to tar Edwards with the brush of Bill Clinton and the Lewinsky scandal. "He is absolutely a clone of Bill Clinton. I wonder if that man that made the sheep over in Scotland might have worked on Edwards for Clinton," Faircloth told CNN. But many voters, including some Republicans, said that the cynical attack ads made them vote *for* the underdog Edwards, who looked fresh and idealistic by comparison. He ran on such platforms as building more schools and hiring more teachers, regulating HMOs, and defending the textile business; he even had nice things to say about his opponent's mentor, Jesse Helms. The youthful Edwards won, 51-47.

In the Senate, Edwards was known both for having a friendly and pleasing manner and for being persuasive in debates (and two years into his term, *People* magazine would name him 2000's "sexiest politician alive"). Al Gore thought highly enough of him to count him as a runner-up as a vice presidential nominee. He was generally regarded as one of the South's New Democrats, with what the *Almanac of American Politics* calls a voting record in the "moderate to conservative range" among Senate Democrats, although the *National Journal* gave him a considerably more liberal ranking, reflective of a genuinely mixed voting record.

On domestic issues, Edwards supported efforts to increase use of generic drugs, and cosponsored with McCain and Kennedy a bill regulating HMOs. He strongly opposed privatizing Social Security and extending the Bush tax cuts; supported reproductive rights, reform of drug laws, and a pathway to citizenship for illegal immigrants; and had a mixed record on guns and free trade. He was less corporate-friendly than the Clinton New Democrats, but not by all that much. He took an active role, for example, in supporting the consolidation of the banking and financial services industries. In 1999, he voted for "financial modernization legislation" which, as CNN described it, "effectively eliminates Depression-era firewalls that prevented the outright merger of commercial banks, insurance companies and brokerage firms." The legislation, supported by Clinton, would "benefit investors and merger-minded institutions," while "consumer advocates assailed the deal for putting profits above the interests of the average customer."

The VP and the DLC

There has been some controversy over whether Edwards was once a member of the Democratic Leadership Council—of which no better description can be found than that offered by *Black Commentator* editors Glen Ford and Peter Gamble:

> Bill Clinton humiliated, abused, bamboozled and, finally, eviscerated the base of the Democratic Party in the Nineties. His biggest victories were NAFTA and welfare reform, both achieved with overwhelming Republican support. Clinton's tenure marked the triumph of the Democratic Leadership Council, the southern-born, white male-pandering, union-bashing, corporate wing of the Party. Republicans did a great service to Clinton and his vice president, Al Gore, by labeling them "liberals"—perversely confirming that the DLC had succeeded in moving the national Democratic Party rightward. Clinton unleashed the dogs of Wall Street to inflate the speculative bubble that obligingly waited for him to leave office before bursting—a legacy of corporate mayhem, a marauding World Trade Organization, massive de-industrialization, merger madness, and obscene growth in CEO compensation that George Bush eagerly builds upon.[4]

Edwards says he was never a card-carrying member. But while in Congress, Edwards was a founder of the New Democrat Coalition, itself an affiliate of the DLC, which greeted news of this organization on March 13, 2000 with this statement: "Though US Senators have always played a key role in the DLC and the New Democrat movement, we're pleased to see that nine senators have taken the formal step of organizing a New Democrat Coalition to work with the existing sixty-four-member NDC in the House. The founding members of the Senate NDC include: Joe Lieberman (CT), Evan Bayh (IN), Mary Laundrieu (LA), John Edwards (NC), John Breaux (LA), Chuck Robb (VA), Blanche Lambert Lincoln (AR), Bob Kerrey (NE) and Bob Graham (FL)." In 2002, he was a featured speaker at the DLC's "National Conversation" in New York. With the Enron scandal close at hand and the stock market falling, he did call for greater accountability from corporations as well as government, but couched his critique in a way that cozied up to the DLC—and implied, through his use of the first person plural, that he was one of them: "A decade ago, the DLC said we should expand opportunity and demand responsibility. Now the president is borrowing our words and says he wants to usher in a responsibility era. . . . I know President Bush likes to steal ideas from us—but Mr. President, if you're not going to use that word 'responsibility,' we'd like to have it back."[5]

In the summer of 2003, John Edwards's relationship to DLC people and ideas was confirmed by *The New Republic* (which certainly ought to know):

> Finally, like Clinton in 1992, Edwards has established himself as the candidate of the centrist Democratic Leadership Council (DLC), although he has no interest in pigeon-holing himself with that label. *TNR* contributor Bruce Reed, who served as Clinton's domestic policy adviser before

becoming president of the DLC, is an influential Edwards adviser who helped shape the three recent speeches. And, while Edwards was stumping in New Hampshire over the weekend, Reed was hosting a meeting of New Democrats in Philadelphia, where he released the DLC's "New Agenda for the Next Decade," a document filled with policies that Edwards now talks about on the stump, including the creation of a new domestic intelligence agency; tax proposals to help the middle class buy a home, pay for college, and save for retirement; a plan to "stop the scandal of excessive CEO pay"; support for after-school programs; and an attack on corporate welfare.[6]

At the same time, David Broder, writing in the *Washington Post*, noted: "Edwards was not a DLC member, but only because he saw that [primary rivals] Lieberman and Kerry had a better claim on its support. His policy views are perfectly compatible with the group's."

At the 2004 Boston convention, in his speech accepting the vice presidential nomination, Edwards repeated his "two Americas" theme: "We have much work to do, because the truth is, we still live in a country where there are two different Americas—one, for all of those people who have lived the American dream and don't have to worry, and another for most Americans, everybody else who struggle to make ends meet every single day. It doesn't have to be that way." But when it came to policy matters he hewed closely to the DLC line that John Kerry too had embraced as part of his strategy—clearly wrongheaded, as it turns out—to get elected. He promised all the usual improvements—in education, in healthcare—but these would be accomplished not through any sweeping systemic changes or bold government programs, such as publicly funded preschools or single-payer healthcare, but the DLC favorite, "tax credits."

"First, we're going to help you pay for your healthcare by having a tax break and healthcare reform that can save you up to $1,000 on your premiums. We're going to help you cover the rising costs of child care with a tax credit up to $1,000 so that your kids have a place to go when you're at work that they're safe and well taken care of. If your child—if your child wants to be the first in your family to go to college, we're going to give you a tax break on up to $4,000 in tuition."

Even for the middle classes, tax credits are a timid and anemic solution to the problems caused by the nation's lack of basic social programs. For the poor, they are useless: What good is a tax credit if you don't have an income—or have one so low that it barely qualifies for income taxes at all?

Edwards did go on to speak eloquently about poverty. "We can also do something about 35 million Americans who live in poverty every day. And here's why we shouldn't just talk about, but do something about the millions of Americans who live in poverty: because it is wrong. And we have a moral responsibility to lift those families up. I mean, the very idea that in a country of our wealth and our prosperity, we have children going to bed hungry? We have children who don't have the clothes to keep them warm? We have millions of Americans who work full time every day to support their families, working for minimum wage, and still live in poverty. It's wrong. These are men and women who are living up to their bargain. They're working hard, they're supporting their families. Their families are doing their part; it's time we did our part."

But again, the policy proposals were weak and predictable: "raise the minimum wage" (to a level where, if everyone works two or three jobs, a family might just make enough money to qualify for a tax credit) and "finish the job on welfare reform" (for which he seems to see no downside), and "bring good-paying jobs to the places where we need them the most." And it wouldn't cost much to fund such limited changes, so rich people and corporate interests need not fear: the wealthy would simply return to paying the already low tax rates of the Clinton years, and corporations would just have to stop cheating (or stop getting caught). "We are going to keep and protect the tax cuts for 98 percent of Americans— 98 percent. We're going to roll back the tax cuts for the wealthiest Americans. And we're going to close corporate loopholes. We're going to cut government contractors and wasteful spending." The all-powerful tax incentives would also be used to "create good-paying jobs in America again"; Edwards promised to "get rid of tax cuts for companies who are outsourcing your jobs"; instead, there would be "tax breaks to American companies that are keeping jobs right here in America."[7]

The Candidate

Those now supporting John Edwards as a liberal alternative are eager to separate him from the likes of the Democratic Leadership Council. A posting at the Edwards Supporters Central blog states:

Some people assume that while John Edwards was
in the Senate he was a member of the Democratic
Leadership Council, or the DLC (let's just say that
we at Democrats United for Edwards are not fans
of the DLC and we consider many of their members
to be spineless hacks). Edwards was considered to
be more "moderate" in his early Senate days (he
represented a solid red state) but he has always been
guided by the same core values. Although he was
heavily courted, John Edwards never joined the
DLC.[8]

Try as they might, however, they cannot erase
Edwards's ties to the DLC in the past (the "courting"
clearly worked both ways), though he was neither as conservative nor as cynical as the worst of the Council's
"spineless hacks." No amount of wishful thinking, for
that matter, will produce evidence of a radical transformation on Edwards's part. Still, he has indeed moved to
the left on several issues—in some cases, far enough left
to distinguish himself from Clinton and Obama, who can
also be found playing so-called populist cards when it
seems politically expedient to do so.

With what seems by now a characteristic blend of
shrewdness and sincerity—a combination of a genuine
concern for those in his "other America" with a consciousness of the mood of the political moment—Edwards
appears to have set out, soon after the 2004 election, to
position himself in the ample space that existed to the left
of the presumptive leader in the 2008 Democratic primary
race, Hillary Clinton. (In fact, the conventional wisdom
on the 2004 primary was that Edwards's slow-starting

campaign took off only when he began to talk about the two Americas—so once again, what was good for the less fortunate was also good for him.)

Immediately after the 2004 campaign, Edwards—who had already lost his teenaged son to a car accident in 1996—faced a personal crisis when Elizabeth Edwards was diagnosed with breast cancer. Edwards took a position as director of the University of North Carolina at Chapel Hill's Center on Poverty, Work and Opportunity. He created and paid for the "College for Everyone" program to fund the first year of college for several hundred students in rural North Carolina. He continued to travel, making speeches at union events, visiting Hurricane Katrina victims, and going to college campuses to educate students about poverty.

It was during this period that Edwards undertook activities that stand to become the worst liabilities in his campaign. First, in the fall of 2005, he took a job with the hedge fund Fortress Investment Group, where he remained as an "adviser" until he announced his candidacy in December 2006. Some months later, reports surfaced in the press showing that during his time at Fortress, the firm had significantly expanded its business in subprime lending—the high-risk mortgages that have financially destroyed so many poor and working-class people, and were blamed for a 42 percent increase in home foreclosures in 2006 alone. It had also incorporated its funds in the Cayman Islands to avoid paying US taxes. According to the *Washington Post*, "At the time of his hiring, he said, he sought assurance that Fortress was not involved in predatory lending, union-busting or dismantling companies. His work, he said, involved giving the firm insight into Washington and observing trends he saw while traveling the country." But records also showed that Fortress employees and their family members had donated some $167,000 to the Edwards campaign, the largest amount from a single company. And the story broke in the same month that Edwards had announced a plan to protect homeowners from "the shameful lending practices that are compromising our strength as a nation"—which once again, could be taken as proof either of his independence or his hypocrisy.

Edwards also engaged in some other activities in 2005 and 2006 that are now raising uncomfortable questions. He formed a non-profit organization called the Center for Promise and Opportunity, dedicated, according to its mission statement, "to exploring new ways to expand opportunity and realize the promise of our country for all Americans." A sister charity founded by Edwards, the Promise and Opportunity Foundation, gave out the college scholarships in North Carolina, and was entirely aboveboard. But the DC-based Center, which shared offices with Edwards's political PACs, seems primarily to have served Edwards's political aspirations. As documented by the *New York Times* in June, the officers belonged to his political staff and the Center helped pay for Edwards's trips to early primary states. "The $1.3 million the group raised and spent in 2005 paid for travel, including Mr. Edwards's 'Opportunity Rocks' tour of ten college campuses, consultants and a Web operation. In addition, some $540,000 went for the 'exploration of new ideas,' according to tax filings." Because donations were not tax deductible, Edwards didn't have to disclose the identity of the donors, which he subsequently declined to do when asked by the paper. "I can't say what Mr. Edwards did was wrong," Marcus S. Owens, a lawyer in private practice in Washington who once ran the IRS division in charge of nonprofits, told the *Times*. "But he was working right up to the line. Who knows whether he stepped or stumbled over it. But he was close enough that if a wind was blowing hard, he'd fall over it." The article, which played loose in attributing motives (Edwards, its lede suggested, used the Center "to keep alive his public profile without the benefit of a presidential campaign that could finance his travels and pay for his political staff") but was sound enough in its facts, drew another indignant response from Edwards's overly sarcastic deputy campaign manager Jonathan Price—"Perish the thought: people involved in politics actually trying to improve peoples' lives"—and outraged responses on the web, which accused the *Times* of everything from libel to facism. But a pragmatic and telling comment appeared on the blog of *The Left Observer*'s Doug Henwood:

"The Democratic Party cannot win unless it has a clean candidate. If Edwards is nominated, the Justice Department will hold a very public investigation into this. Imagine the headlines about the Democratic nominee and corruption.

"The Democrats . . . need someone who is above suspicion of corruption. They need someone who can point to the dirty deeds of the GOP with without fear that they will point back at him."

The chances of finding a candidate who is "above suspicion of corruption" may run from slim to none, depending on how you define "corruption": if it includes selling out to corporate lobbyists in return for campaign contributions, Edwards still looks somewhat cleaner than either Clinton or Obama. Still, questionable operations like the Center for Promise and Opportunity stand to be deadly for Edwards, whose already scant chance at winning the nomination rests, in large part, in his appeal to voters on "moral" grounds.

Domestic Programs

Edwards's poverty reduction program is a mix of ideas advocated over the years by the party centrists, with a few imaginative touches and some stirring rhetoric. In one way or another, these are all good ideas. They have been tried off and on since the New Deal with varying degrees of success.

Edwards would raise the minimum wage to "at least $7.50 an hour." He has a jobs program for the unemployed that sounds limited and vague. He would create a million "stepping stone jobs for workers who take responsibility"—minimum wage jobs lasting up to twelve months, and in return, "workers must show up and work hard, stay off drugs, not commit any crimes, and pay child support." (Dennis Kucinich, in contrast, wants to put people without jobs to work rebuilding America's crumbling public infrastructure—bridges, tunnels, roads—at a time when many politicians in both parties are desiring to sell them off; his program would put people of New Orleans to work rebuilding their own city and its water defenses.) Edwards, who has courted unions with considerable success (one state AFL-CIO head introduced him as "a blue collar president for a blue collar America"), also supports stronger labor laws, including the Employee Free Choice Act, which would remove barriers to organizing.

He favors housing vouchers—again, numbering one million—that will let poor people live where they want, the idea being to phase out public housing, and create more income-integrated neighborhoods. A million better homes, like a million jobs, are good things—but there are 37 million people living in poverty in the United States. More significant, despite his history, is his pledge to fight predatory lending practices. Beyond that, for low-income workers there are "Work Bonds"—a $500 match for savings—and expanded tax credits, especially for working adults without children, who "are the only Americans living in poverty who pay income and payroll taxes"; these would average $750. Again, good ideas, and nicely specific—but not a lot of money. It's hard to see, in fact, how all of these proposals would add up to Edwards's ambitious "National Goal," which is "to end poverty within thirty years." The model Edwards cites is telling, and not all that encouraging: "In 1999, Tony Blair announced a twenty-year goal to end child poverty in Great Britain and he has already reduced child poverty by 17 percent." This is not much progress for Blair in eight years—or nearly halfway—into his projected twenty-year period, and he was only targeting *child* poverty, in a country with a lower poverty rate than the United States.

In two areas—healthcare, the debt—Edwards's proposals exemplify the ambiguity of his policies. In both cases, proponents say that they may seem like small steps forward—reflecting what is politically possible in today's conservative climate—but they could become the opening salvos in a wider more radical future. Or, of course, they might remain relatively timid reforms.

The most interesting, and conceivably most practical, is a scheme for dealing with consumer debt that is drowning the American middle class. When it comes to domestic issues that pit the interests of large corporations against those of ordinary Americans, few equal the exploding crisis in consumer debt, particularly credit card debt. And here Edwards is the one candidate who has been willing to tackle this problem head on. The candidates' general reluctance is hardly surprising, since the same financial institutions that engage in predatory lending practices constitute their largest contributors, as well as what is possibly the most powerful lobby in all of Washington.

More than half of Americans carry credit card debt; the average household debt to credit cards is about $10,000, and the average annual interest paid is over $1,300. According to the Federal Reserve, consumer credit card debt in the United States totals $880 billion; this figure, adjusted to current dollars, has increased a hundred-fold in the last forty years. About 40 percent of American households spend more than they earn each year. These numbers, huge by any standard, represent a growing factor in the nation's questionable economic future.

Those carrying credit card debt are not limited to self-indulgent spenders unwilling to forego luxuries: "The Plastic Safety Net," a 2005 survey of low and middle income households conducted by Demos and the Center for Responsible Lending, found that declines in public and private benefit programs—health coverage, pensions, and unemployment insurance among them—have contributed to the growth in credit card debt. For example, 29 percent of households surveyed reported that medical expenses made up a portion of their current balances.[9] With the housing market in its current shaky state, credit cards are increasingly being used to buy housing as well as other consumer products.

Today many credit card companies are owned by big banks. While these are regulated by the federal government, the regulation only pertains to their profitability. Fairness or consumer protection does not enter the picture. As a result, the credit card business is literally unregulated at the national level; the credit card companies can charge—or change—interest rates at will. The business may be regulated by state law, but two states, South Dakota and Delaware, have the weakest consumer laws, and no control over interest rates—so credit card companies set up shop and run national and international operations from these safe havens.

To make the situation worse, the new bankruptcy law that went into effect in 2005 makes it much harder to declare bankruptcy, and requires filers, including those with very modest incomes, to pay off much of their credit card debt regardless. Initiated in 2001, the law was vigorously opposed by consumer groups and unions, and championed by Bush, whose largest campaign contributor had been the credit card giant MBNA (which subsequently merged with Bank of America). On an initial vote in 2001, it also won the support of thirty-six Senate Democrats, including not only Edwards but other current presidential candidates Joe Biden, Hillary Clinton, and John Edwards, while only Dennis Kucinich and Chris Dodd voted against it.

When it came up for a second vote in 2005, Edwards

was gone from the Senate. Obama, Kucinich, and Dodd voted against it; Biden (who represents credit card central, the state of Delaware) voted for it; and Hillary Clinton was the only member of the Senate who didn't vote on the measure.

Now, most of the presidential candidates simply are not confronting the credit card issue. For Republicans, this is a predictable state of affairs. But the top three Democrats' relationship to powerful lenders is more complicated. Despite his 2001 yes vote on the bankruptcy legislation, John Edwards is now the only candidates now taking up the issue—relying, in large part, on the analysis and ideas of Elizabeth Warren, a Harvard professor and fierce critic of consumer lenders. Warren argues that existing systems are inadequate to control the credit card crisis, and need to be reformed through legislation. "The current problem is that the Federal Reserve, the Office of the Controller of the Currency, and other financial regulatory institutions are not currently charged to protect consumer safety," she explains. "The primary responsibility of the regulatory agencies is to assure the profitability of the banks and other lending institutions, not to protect consumers from deceptive and unsafe products."

In a speech on his campaign theme of "the Two Americas" at Cooper Union in New York City in June 2007, Edwards proposed "setting up a new consumer commission to be called the Family Savings and Credit Commission . . . [to] deal with all financial services—credit cards, mortgages, car loans, check-cashers, payday loans, investment accounts, and more. It will ban the most abusive terms and make sure consumers understand the others." To many, this will seem an overly roundabout way of regulation, and one that doesn't get at the high interest rates. But Edwards also more directly pledged to "pass strong national laws protecting us against the worst abuses in credit markets: predatory mortgages, abusive credit card terms, and payday loans with interest rates of 300 percent or higher." Elizabeth Warren is less than sanguine about the chances of such legislation getting through. "The problem with instituting a new usury law is politics. The credit industry hires a lot more lobbyists than the consumer advocacy groups, and the creditors have been almost uniformly opposed to any usury laws." All told, in 2006, financial and credit card companies gave $7 million in campaign contributions, and banks $25 million, to candidates of both parties, according to opensecrets.org. The top recipient, with $378,000, was Hillary Clinton. Barak Obama has also built a reputation for fundraising from the big banks and financial services firms. Edwards, whose biggest funders are lawyers, might have a bit more independence. He also has a lot less money.

Healthcare is certain to figure as a major factor in the 2008 presidential election. It ranked second only to Iraq in a recent Gallup poll on top priorities for the president and Congress and was first among domestic priorities. Another poll, commissioned by SEIU, the healthcare workers' union, found that 82 percent of likely voters in the first four caucus and primary states agree that "everyone has a right to quality, affordable healthcare coverage." (This included 92 percent of Democratic voters and, more surprisingly, 72 percent of Republicans.) "Universal healthcare" has become the grand Democratic slogan found on every campaign website and repeated in every stump speech and debate. But the phrase itself is misleading—most often, it actually means "universal health insurance." While the plans do outline some modest and not altogether meaningless reforms, especially when it comes to care for children, most are designed to preserve—and even benefit—the twin scourges of the US healthcare system: the insurance companies and the pharmaceutical industry. With the exception of the acknowledged mavericks Dennis Kucinich and Mike Gravel, no one has suggested anything resembling a single-payer national healthcare system (that is, one that is managed and administered by the federal government), which would boot out the rapacious middlemen of the insurance industry and reign in Big Pharma—the primary obstacles to quality, affordable healthcare in this country. Instead, most Democratic candidates are proposing to subsidize private insurance purchases for the uninsured, which would most likely wind up bringing the insurance companies billions in new income, while in some cases failing to serve the neediest individuals.

But Edwards's plan has one facet missing from those of the other leaders, which has been seized upon by hopeful single-payer supporters. He described his plan at a forum on healthcare held in Nevada in March 2007:

> Basically what we do is cover all Americans. In my plan there's shared responsibilities. The employers are required to either cover their employees or to pay into a fund that will help pay for coverage for their employees. The government plays an important role. The government will set up healthcare markets all across America, and in each of those markets if you're the consumer, you can go in and choose what your healthcare plan would be. Some

of the choices are private insurers, and then one choice is a government plan, basically a Medicare Plus plan. And the idea is to determine whether Americans actually want a private insurer or whether they'd rather have government run Medicare Plus kind of single-payer plan. And we'll find out over time which way people go.

"It is true that single-payer healthcare systems in the world dramatically reduce costs and significantly reduce administrative costs, particularly compared to private insurers," Edwards said in Nevada. "It's also true that a lot of people who are listening to this forum like the health insurance they have now and would like to keep it. And my judgment is, number one, to get it done so that we don't spend another decade arguing about whether we keep the system we have now or actually have universal healthcare. I think this system, my proposal, a truly universal plan, a bold plan, but doesn't go directly to single-payer, can be accomplished. I think it can be accomplished politically. I think we can get support from across the political spectrum and will accomplish a lot of what we want to do. Second, it does give people choice. And I think Americans have become accustomed to having choice, and I think they want to be able to choose what their healthcare plan is. Now, it may be that that gravitates towards a single-payer plan because they will have the Medicare plus the choices. And if that's the case, then the whole system can go in that direction. But you'll decide that. Consumers will decide that."

While Edwards was here speaking to a particularly liberal audience—the forum was sponsored by the Center for American Progress and the SEIU—it's easy to see why his plan would raise hopes. What this boils down to is having a Medicare type plan compete with private plans. Steffi Woolhandler, Harvard professor and co-founder of Physicians for a National Health Program, says flatly: "Edwards's plan is not going to work. We know there is not going to be fair competition between Medicare and the private plans. You have to take on the private health insurance industry and tell them—you are out of here. This is an entitlement program like traditional Medicare or Social Security. We are going to get the administrative efficiencies you get from running it as a single program and use that to expand coverage. That's what you have to do."

Foreign Policy

During his years in the Senate, John Edwards voted for the USA PATRIOT Act. He also not only voted for the Iraq War Resolution—he co-sponsored it, along with Lieberman. On October 10, 2002, Edwards said "Almost no one disagrees with these basic facts: that Saddam Hussein is a tyrant and a menace; that he has weapons of mass destruction and that he is doing everything in his power to get nuclear weapons; that he has supported terrorists; that he is a grave threat to the region, to vital allies like Israel, and to the United States; and that he is thwarting the will of the international community and undermining the United Nations' credibility."

In fact, the people who disagreed with these basic facts were in the CIA, and their doubts were contained in a classified report available to Congress before the 2002 war vote. But Edwards said it was not necessary to read the report, since as a member of the Senate Intelligence committee he was getting information directly from intelligence officers. "I had the information I needed," he later said. "I just voted wrong."

Now, as his website describes it, "Edwards has issued a comprehensive proposal to end the war in Iraq—starting today: It calls on Congress to use its funding power to block President Bush's escalation, immediately begin withdrawing troops by capping funding and requiring complete withdrawal of all combat troops in 12 to 18 months." In debates and in the press he has been critical of the Congress—and his rivals in it—for not acting more aggressively. When House Democrats voted for partial war funding in May, Edwards said in a statement: "This is not a compromise; it is a concession." This proposal may not give George Bush all the money he wants, but it gives him all the money he needs to continue his surge and keep the war going." Senate Majority Leader Harry Reid complained that "the former senator no longer has to worry about voting. . . . We're legislating, and he's campaigning."

In part Edwards's views towards the Middle East have been influenced by his concern for Israel, a nation he strongly supports. "As long as the Palestinian leadership fails to end terror, Israel has a right to take measures to defend itself. Such defensive measures are not the cause of terrorism—they are the response to terrorism," he said in January 2004. In October of the same year he took a tough line on Iran. "It's important for America to confront the situation in Iran, because Iran is an enormous threat to Israel and to the Israeli people."

At a conference in Herzliya, Israel, in January 2007, Edwards was asked: "Would you be prepared, if diplomacy failed, to take further action against Iran? I think there is cynicism about the ability of diplomacy to work in this situation. Secondly, you as a grassroots person, who has an understanding of the American people, is there understanding of this threat across US?" Edwards replied:

> My analysis of Iran is if you start with the president of Iran coming to the UN in New York denouncing America and his extraordinary and nasty statements about the Holocaust and goal of wiping Israel off map, married with his attempts to obtain nuclear weapons over a long period of time, they are buying time. They are the foremost state sponsors of terrorism. If they have nuclear weapons, other states in the area will want them, and this is unacceptable.
>
> As to what to do, we should not take anything off the table. More serious sanctions need to be undertaken, which cannot happen unless Russia and China are seriously on board, which has not happened up until now. I would not want to say in advance what we would do, and what I would do as president, but there are other steps that need to be taken. For example, we need to support direct engagement with Iranians, we need to be tough. But I think it is a mistake strategically to avoid engagement with Iran.
>
> As to the American people, this is a difficult question. The vast majority of people are concerned about what is going on in Iraq. This will make the American people reticent toward going

for Iran. But I think the American people are smart if they are told the truth, and if they trust their president. So Americans can be educated to come along with what needs to be done with Iran.[10]

A few weeks later, in a Washington interview with Ezra Klein for the *American Prospect*, Edwards appeared to back off. He told the reporter Bush should be "negotiating directly" with Iran and proposed an "economic package" should be offered as an enticement to avoid "serious economic sanctions." Klein pushed the question: "So, I just want to get it very clear, you think that attacking Iran would be a bad idea?" "I think it would have very bad consequences," Edwards responded. Klein asked, "So when you said that all options are on the table?" "It would be foolish for any American president to ever take any option off the table," said Edwards.

It remains unclear, in fact, how much Edwards has changed in his broad attitudes toward military interventions abroad as a matter of policy, and how much he simply opposes the failed Iraq War and the suffering it causes daily. Paul Begala, the Democratic consultant close to Hillary Clinton, depicted Edwards as a born-again peacenik: "In 2002, he sounded like General Patton. Now he sounds like Mahatma Gandhi."

The Road Ahead

By July of 2007, Edwards's numbers were dropping. According to most (though not all) polls, he was hovering somewhere around 15 percent, with Barack Obama generally in the high 20s and Hillary Clinton pushing 40.[11] Some commentators have noted that Obama was the unknown variable when Edwards began, three years ago, to carve out a position for himself to the left of Clinton. Without him in the race, Edwards could claim most of the substantial bloc of voters who find her too conservative or just too Hillary, and the numbers today might look quite different.

In any case, Edwards's fortunes will be made on how voters in the early primary states respond to his platform—especially, perhaps, in Iowa, where his putatively populist stand looks to have deeper appeal, and where he maintains numbers higher than in the national polls. In a piece in *Men's Vogue*, Joe Hagan describes Edwards campaigning in Iowa as "a populist Adonis, a golden god of a Southern Democrat," but wonders if the polished image can play with the "pale, stern-faced farmers in plaid shirts and modestly coiffed housewives" of rural America, concluding that for them, the hair might be "looking a little too good": "It's the hair versus the message and, at this moment, it's hard to know which will win."

NOTES

1. See http://www.truthandpolitics.org/top-rates.php] [http://www.cbpp.org/10-16-03tax.htm.
2. Goodwyn, *A Short History of the Agrarian Revolt in America*, New York: Oxford University Press, 1978, p. viii.
3. See http://projects.newsobserver.com/dome/profiles/john_Edwards.
4. See http://www.blackcommentator.com/57/57_cover_clark.html.
5. See http://www.dlc.org/ndol_ci.cfm?contentid=250711&kaid=106&subid=122.
6. See http://www.tnr.com/doc.mhtml?i=20030811&s=lizza081103.
7. See http://www.washingtonpost.com/wp-dyn/articles/A22230-2004Jul28.html.
8. See http://edwardssupportercentral.blogspot.com/2007/04/misconceptions-never-member-of-dlc.html.
9. See http://www.demos.org/pub654.cfm.

10. See http://www.rawstory.com/news/2007/Edwards_Iran_must_know_world _wont_0123.html.
11. See http://www.pollingreport.com/wh08dem.htm.

Because He Was Right: Dennis Kucinich

ELI SANDERS AND DAN SAVAGE

Is America ready for its first vegan president?

Please.

Maybe its first woman president. Perhaps a black president. Possibly even a Latino president. And, as Chris Rock pointed out, we've got a retarded president right now. But a guy who faults a cheeseburger on two counts, the meat and the cheese? A *vegan* president? No fucking way. Don't be retarded.

And most certainly not this particular vegan, Ohio congressman Dennis Kucinich. This is a candidate who announces, on national television, that he would refuse to shoot a Hellfire missile at Osama bin Laden if given the opportunity; a guy who prattles on about the interconnectedness of humanity and his plans for creating a cabinet-level Department of Peace; a man who brags about the wonderfully low blood pressure his animal-cruelty-free diet has brought him (memo to the Kucinich campaign: Americans like their leaders carnivorous *and* on the verge of cardiac arrest, thank you very much—see, for example, our last two presidents, Bill Clinton and Dick Cheney).

Sure, it might be unfair, a cosmic and karmic injustice even, that Kucinich, who was more right about the Iraq War than most Democrats (and, for the record, more right than one of the meat-eating authors of this vegan-bashing profile), now has less chance of being president than US troops have of stumbling across those alleged Iraqi WMDs.

But that's the way we roll here in America.

This is a country in which 41 percent of people still believe that Saddam Hussein was responsible for 9/11. This is a country in which some people still believe that there is some sort of dignified way out of Iraq—"home with honor" is how the pollsters and strategists describe the widespread sentiment—and, delusional or not, these Americans don't see much "honor" in our troops marching out of the Middle East on the orders of a five-foot-seven, turn-the-other-cheek waif who flashes peace signs without irony and wouldn't eat a steak with the boys once they're back home.

None of this stops Kucinich, however. Long odds never have. He soldiers on (sorry, too militaristic?), making his second consecutive run at the White House, and no more likely to win this time around than in 2004—although, as he points out at every opportunity, times have changed considerably since his last go at the presidency, when he received just one percent of the delegate votes at the 2004 Democratic Convention in Boston.

"The American people are ready for peace and they know I was right," Kucinich said during an interview in New Hampshire in early June, after a CNN debate that gave him relatively little airtime and saw him positioned, on the stage, at the furthest left fringe of the seven other Democratic presidential hopefuls.

Because he's a peace candidate who nevertheless loves a political fight, Kucinich followed up his comments with a jab at the other Democrat contenders who supported the war. "Others," he said, in reference to Hillary Clinton and John Edwards, "were wrong."

Yeah, Hillary and John were wrong, Dennis, just like most of the American people—you know, the *American* people, those flag-waving meat-eaters you're trying to talk into voting for you. We're guessing they don't like being reminded that they were wrong anymore than your opponents do.

Kucinich, sixty, has long been an "everyone else is wrong" type of guy, the type of politician who strikes a certain type of liberal as totally righteous for his unwillingness to compromise. But he strikes a lot of other liberals—a clear majority, as evidenced by his vote totals in liberal-dominated Democratic primaries—as obnoxious and inflexible to an agenda-hobbling degree.

It's hard to find anyone, however, who doesn't see him as exceptionally driven.

Kucinich was born in Cleveland, Ohio, in 1946, to a working-class family that saw some hard times; on occasion, his family was forced to sleep in cars. He made his first attempt at public office at the age of twenty, filing a petition to run for a spot on the Cleveland City Council despite the fact that he couldn't legally vote yet. The year was 1967, and at the time he was still a sophomore at Cleveland State University, studying toward a degree in communications. Kucinich didn't succeed in that first run for office, but just over two years later he did, joining the city council at the age of twenty-three. If that span of three years shows the mark of an ambitious and unrelenting personality, it was only the beginning: Three years later, Kucinich ran for Congress as Democrat. He lost, but within two years the man who had defeated him, Republican William E. Minshall, Jr., retired. Kucinich then ran again for the seat. When he didn't get the Democratic nomination for his second attempt at Minshall's seat, Kucinich ran as an independent.

He lost. Again. A few years passed, and then, readjusting his sights, Kucinich ran for mayor of Cleveland. In that race, being the stubbornly populist son of a Cleveland truck driver played to his advantage. Kucinich won, becoming, at age thirty-one, the youngest big-city mayor in American history up to that time, and earning himself national attention as the "Boy Mayor of Cleveland." He proceeded to make more history, not all of it the kind an ambitious young politician would hope for. Most famously, in order to keep electricity rates low in his city, Kucinich refused to sell off Cleveland's municipal power company, Muni Light, to a larger power company that was using all of its political and economic leverage to try to force a sale. Although Kucinich succeeded in his crusade against the larger power company, his victory came at a very high price. To hang on to Muni Light, Cleveland was forced to default on some of its bonds.

Because of this, under Kucinich's tenure as mayor, Cleveland became the first American city to go into financial default since the Great Depression. (And this on top of some other notorious Kucinich accomplishments: his banning of nuns from City Hall and his sacking of a well-regarded police chief via press conference on Good Friday—both of which probably contributed to his having to wear a bullet-proof vest to throw out the first pitch at an Indians game in 1978.) It will not surprise, then, that it was during this time that Kucinich became tagged with his "Dennis the Menace" label—a moniker that, consciously or not, Kucinich has succeeded in keeping in circulation for nearly thirty years.

Kucinich himself has described his rocky mayorality in Cleveland as "absolute chaos," and others have tended to agree. Due in large part to his temperament while in office, he placed seventh on an authoritative list of the ten worst big-city mayors since 1820. While mayor, Kucinich did manage to survive a recall attempt (by two hundred votes), but when reelection time came around in 1979, he was solidly defeated. He slunk off to promote a French book written about his tenure, *L'Enfant Terrible*, and told people he was working on a novelized memoir about his experience.

Then came his fifteen years of wandering in the political wilderness—his time as a college lecturer, his stint as a TV reporter, his flight to Los Angeles, his trouble paying his mortgage, his friendship with the actress Shirley MacLaine and with her "spiritual facilitator," Chris Griscom, whose Light Institute, located near Santa Fe, New Mexico, listed Kucinich as a client in the 1990s, according to a *Washingtonian* profile from the time. That *Washingtonian* profile quoted the institute's marketing director as saying the Light Institute helps people "expand their consciousness" and "get in touch with their inner child," along with helping them expand the "multi-dimensional and multi-incarnational" aspects of their identities.

In the *Washingtonian* profile, Kucinich laughed off a question about whether he had come to believe in past lives, answering the query with a joke about the many public reincarnations of some politicians. What exactly Kucinich believes about reincarnation has been a source of speculation ever since his Light Institute days, but in the end, it probably doesn't matter much (except to late-night comics) whether, during his sojourn away from the campaign trail, Kucinich was a student of actual man-dies-and-comes-back-to-life-as-an-insect reincarnation, or just a student of the more run of the mill, into-the-wilderness-and-back, political reincarnation. Something clearly worked.

In 1994, with big fundraising help from MacClaine, Kucinich began his second political life, winning a seat in the Ohio state senate. His stock was on the rise as the passage of time vindicated him: It turned out that Kucinich's financial brinksmanship in the Muni Light affair had saved Cleveland citizens millions of dollars. In his run for state senate his campaign posters featured a light bulb and the phrase, "Because he was right." When he ran for Congress, in 1996, his posters said, "Light up Congress." And in 1998, in a final bit of political absolution, Kucinich was honored by the Cleveland city council for "having the courage and foresight" to hang on to Muni Light despite paying the ultimate political price at the time.

When Kucinich talks, today, as if he is convinced that he will be proven right eventually on every issue, and campaigns in New Hampshire and other battleground states as if "Because he was right: Iraq edition" will be a winning slogan at the presidential level, this experience can't be far from his mind.

Whether he's just reliving glory days or is actually onto something, there's no doubt that Kucinich's win in 1996 was a bona fide moment of glory: His victory in that congressional race was a high point in his march back into public life, and also something of an upset for Democrats at the national level. The seat representing Ohio's 10th District, which includes Cleveland, had been held by a Republican for two terms until Kucinich took it back. He's now held it through five elections. That doesn't mean, however, that he's become more flexible and politically pragmatic in order to make it through six terms in the House.

"Kucinich has lots of energy, he's got a ton of ideas, and he's a little impatient with his colleagues," said Congressman Jim McDermott, who represents Seattle in the House and, like Kucinich, is considered one of the body's most liberal members. The Kucinich brand of impatience, McDermott says, is that of someone who knows he's right and has never learned to tolerate the slow pace of political change.

"He's a guy to take a risk," McDermott told us. "I take some risks myself, so I have respect for people who don't sit and wait for the pack to tell them to do something. But I think his timeline's a little short for this process. I don't disagree with an awful lot of what he's up to, but I think there are ways you might be more successful in getting it done, that's all. The suffering of fools is a talent, and not everybody suffers fools gladly. He believes they oughta move more quickly because this is only going to get worse."

McDermott's ambivalence sums up how a lot of people feel about Kucinich. Right on many issues, but his rhetoric, his personal life, and his way of getting from here to there turns people off. In polls, that's translating into last place finishes; a June poll in New Hampshire found Kucinich getting just 2 percent of the Democratic primary vote. And in terms of press coverage, it's keeping Kucinich in permanent afterthought status. In the spin room immediately after the New Hampshire debate, the Kucinich station, like that of fellow "fringe candidate" Mike Gravel, was completely ignored as reporters and cameramen swarmed around spokespeople for the front-runners: Clinton, Edwards, and Obama. It took the personal intervention of both Kucinich and his bombshell twenty-nine-year-old wife (his third marriage) to draw a crowd, and even then it seemed that most of the attention was due to the irresistibly funny photo-op the couple offers.

Elizabeth Kucinich, the tongue-stud-wearing daughter of a lefty British family, stands six feet tall without heels and looks like a model. In the political realm, where the perception of the superficial can be everything, the sight of such a woman with her arm around the nerdy Kucinich nearly twice her age tends to invite a lot of thoughts about the candidate himself, some of them flattering, but many of them unhelpful to Kucinich's presidential ambitions—thoughts about the insecurities of short men, for example, or the historical tendency of American voters to prefer the tallest guy in the presidential candidate lineup. But the sight of the couple also invites a lot of double-takes, the way seeing Grace Jones with her arm around Al Gore would, and this is something the Kucinich campaign clearly knows. (At a later debate in South Carolina, when Senator Joseph Biden was asked to tell the audience what he likes best about Kucinich, he looked at Kucinich and replied, with a smirk, "Your wife.") It's also something the Kucinich campaign has learned to use to its advantage. At the New Hampshire debate, when Elizabeth entered

Dennis Kucinich

the spin room with Dennis, the problem of his station being ignored was immediately solved. Elizabeth was sporting a jeweled "PEACE" brooch pinned onto her fitted black jacket, showing off perfectly manicured toes that could be seen through the straps of her sleek black high heels and, in a nod to her potential first lady status, wearing a string of pearls. She said nothing, and didn't have to, as the cameras snapped away and the reporters pressed closer. When Kucinich defended his eyebrow-raising debate statement that he wouldn't give the order to "take out" Osama bin Laden with a Hellfire missile ("A peaceful approach is that you don't use assassination," Kucinich told a reporter), Elizabeth nodded, wrapped one of her long arms around his waist, and squeezed him tighter to her side. When he posed for pictures with her, he couldn't wipe the huge, shit-eating grin off his face.

Their love story is quintessential Kucinich. He met her when she came to his office on Capitol Hill two years ago to discuss monetary policy as part of her then new job with the American Monetary Institute—a job she'd taken after a stint at the House of Lords in London, some time working in one of Mother Teresa's homes for poor children in India, and studies in religion and international conflict resolution. At the time of their meeting, Elizabeth's last name was Harper, and the signature line on her emails included a quotation from the film *Kama Sutra*: "Knowing love, I shall allow all things to come and go, to be as supple as the wind and take everything that comes with great courage. My heart is as open as the sky." Kucinich, who had been single for twenty years, and who, in 2003, had told a political forum in New Hampshire that his perfect soulmate would be "fearless in her desire for peace in the world and for universal, single-payer healthcare," found himself awestruck. After the meeting he phoned a friend and exclaimed that he'd met his future wife. Elizabeth also had a love at first sight moment. She later told an interviewer for *The Tampa Tribune* that upon meeting Kucinich, "I felt such hope for America. It made my heart sing."

Shortly after their heart-stopping monetary policy encounter, Elizabeth sent Dennis a business email (including her *Kama Sutra* signature line), and the two began an exchange that led them to discover they would both be in New Mexico at the same time in the near future. They had dinner, spent a night together at Shirley MacLaine's New Mexico home, and a few days later decided to get married.

On the campaign trail Elizabeth has been asked frequently about the height and age differences between herself and her husband, but she prefers to discuss their perfect spiritual union. As she told the London *Sunday Times* in May: "Can you imagine what it would be like to have real love in the White House and a true union between the masculine and the feminine?"

Uh . . . No.

Still, Dennis and Elizabeth do seem a perfect match. In terms of loopy statements related to Kucinich, hers about their "true union between the masculine and the feminine" now rivals Dennis's own famous statement about the universe's "starlit magic" at an international peace conference in Croatia in 2002.

"Spirit merges with matter to sanctify the universe," he explained to the conference crowd. "Matter transcends to return to spirit. The interchangeability of matter and spirit means the starlit magic of the outermost life of our universe becomes the soul-light magic of the innermost life of our self."

Right. Congratulations, Mr. and Mrs. Kucinich. But we're not convinced that your soul-light magic is going to move voters in Iowa—and neither are those who follow every last detail of these races, even down to the appeal of the candidates' wives.

Not long ago, the *New York Times* Sunday Style section devoted an entire article to the question of whether Republican Fred Thompson's beautiful, much younger wife would be viewed as a "trophy wife," and therefore become a political liability if he entered the presidential race. That this question would even be explored in the *Times* was a testament to the perception that Thompson was an otherwise formidable candidate. In 2004, back when John Kerry was still seen as a somewhat-formidable presidential candidate, Theresa Heinz Kerry merited the same type of attention for her unfiltered comments and potentially off-putting sophistication. But Elizabeth Kucinich isn't getting this kind of treatment now. Hardly anyone is ruminating on whether she's viable as a general-election campaign spouse, because hardly anyone seriously believes that she and her husband will make it to the general election. Instead, Elizabeth Kucinich is treated mainly as someone who catches the eye of people like Joe Biden, and who doubles the comedic fodder that her husband's campaign appearances normally provide—as a joke amplifier, in other words, rather than a message amplifier.

But hey, maybe in fifteen years time the Kuciniches will be proven correct. Maybe we'll all wake up one day and realize that matter does, in fact, transcend into spirit, and think to ourselves: You know, a true union between masculine and feminine is just what the White House needs.

In reality, we are far likelier to be saying that about the third and fourth terms of Bill and Hillary than about the first term of Dennis and Elizabeth. But still, you never know. Dennis Kucinich could be right again. As he constantly reminds us: It's happened before.

There is one issue that Kucinich definitely hasn't been right on, at least as far as Democratic primary voters are concerned: Abortion.

He was raised Catholic, and apparently in his adulthood, even as his mind opened to new-age notions and supposedly higher planes of awareness, he remained convinced that a woman's right to choose needed to be severely restricted. In Congress, Kucinich was well aware that this stance didn't play well with his liberal base. He didn't seem to care, but he had enough political sense to try to keep his views quiet.

In 2002, *The Nation* noted that one thing Kucinich wasn't mentioning on his website was his record on reproductive rights. Without much notice, he'd become a darling of the National Right to Life Committee, earning a 0 percent favorable rating from NARAL Pro-Choice America, and amassing a "Henry Hyde-like" anti-choice voting record. You wouldn't have known it back then from his online presence; even now, Kucinich buries reproductive rights at the bottom of the issues page on his campaign website and glosses over his past anti-choice positions this way: "Most Americans, including myself, are uncomfortable with abortions and feel there are too many of them."

But the record is clear. As a congressman, Kucinich has voted to prevent anyone but a parent from taking a teenage girl across state lines for an abortion. He has voted in favor of banning late-term abortions completely, with no exception for the health of the mother. He also voted to make it a crime, punishable by up to two years in prison, for doctors to perform late-term abortions. He opposed giving federal workers coverage for contraceptives in their healthcare plans. He supported Bush's efforts to restrict the use of US family planning funds overseas. He opposed funding for stem cell research. In 1996, he told Planned Parenthood that he did not support the substance of *Roe v. Wade*.

Kucinich claims to be pro-choice now, but as Markos Moulitsas, the founder of the liberal blog DailyKos, noted with disgust on his website earlier this year: "His transformation to being pro-choice happened literally overnight—a week after he announced his 2004 presidential bid. One moment he was virulently anti-choice, the next he was a staunch defender."

Kucinich says that he "evolved." But that supposed evolution involves a flip-flop on abortion even bigger than Mitt Romney's, and strikes many as insincere and politically expedient. Moulitsas, for example, might seem a natural ally of Kucinich since both opposed the Iraq War, but Moulitsas can't stomach Kucinich's stances on abortion. He's written that he now responds to Kucinich's name with one word: "Ugh."

When people tell Kucinich to his face that his chances of winning this season's Democratic nomination (much less the presidency) are slim to none, he always refuses to go along with their skepticism. In April, on *Real Time with Bill Maher*, Maher began his interview with Kucinich by saying: "No one considers that you're really going to win this nomination."

To which Kucinich replied: "Oh, I think I am."

Maher stammered, dumbfounded, and after a long beat of silence, there was a smattering of applause from the audience. But the effect was to make Kucinich look crazy. He doesn't really believe he's going to win, does he?

It's a trap that Kucinich is caught in as a fringe candidate running in his second long-shot race. If he concedes that he's not going to win (again) he has to explain why he's there (again). Vanity? Publicity? To make a symbolic point? Because he likes the great hotel rooms he and Elizabeth get to stay in on the campaign trail? (Well, probably not that last one, given that Kucinich had only raised about $350,000 as of July 1, about one hundred times less than fund raising front-runner Hillary Clinton had; in New Hampshire, Elizabeth and Dennis shared a room at a cheap Super 8 motel near the airport.)

On the flip side, if Kucinch pretends he's actually got a serious chance of winning, he looks, well, out of touch with reality, as he did on *Bill Maher*—and someone who's out of touch with reality is not what Americans, Democrats or Republicans, are looking for after eight years of George W. Bush.

On his show, Maher threw Kucinich a lifeline after telling him he had no chance. "This is what I'm getting at: If you go through your platform, it's like, universal healthcare, ending the drug war, getting serious about the environment, pulling out of Iraq right away—I don't know why you're the crazy one, is what I'm saying. It doesn't seem radical to me."

Why then, Maher wondered, wasn't Kucinich polling higher?

"It's only a matter of time," Kucinich replied.

It may be a matter of a very, very long time. It took Ohio fifteen years to come around and realize Kucinich was right about Muni Light. It's going to take Democrats more than two election cycles to see a vegan peace candidate as electable to the presidency—if they ever do. Democratic primary voters want a winner, especially after the last two elections.

So it doesn't matter that Kucinich is in the right place on a lot of progressive issues—even, belatedly, on abortion—or that he has a lot of fans of his strident opposition to the North American Free Trade Agreement. It doesn't matter that Kucinich is making a lot of noise about impeaching Cheney, even drawing Congressman McDermott in as a co-sponsor of the articles of impeachment he filed against the vice president in the House earlier this year. And it doesn't matter that Kucinich was right on Iraq when other Democrats and a certain sex-advice columnist were wrong—even though, as detractors have pointed out, Kucinich did vote in favor of removing Saddam Hussein from power 1998, back before he became the unflinching "peace candidate" that he is now.

What matters is that Kucinich simply can't win, and has done nothing—in terms of fund raising, poll showings, crowd drawing, or inspiring rhetoric—to demonstrate that he can.

Still, even if it's not his first aim, he does serve one purpose in the primary race. In a party that has long chafed at the rightward tilt of its most marketable candidates, Kucinich, like Ralph Nader, helps to draw the other Democrats' rhetoric and campaign-trail promises back toward the left. Even better, unlike Nader, Kucinich disappears after the primary is over; as a successful Democratic congressman, Kucinich can't very well drop his party affiliation and run as an independent in the general election, siphoning votes away from the chosen Democratic candidate. In 2004, when he lost the race for the nomination, he quietly went back to being a congressman, and he's likely to do the same this time around.

"There are a lot of politicians who try to get to the top by compromising all the time," says Congressman McDermott, who will not be supporting Kucinich. "Dennis is going to make that real tough for the others, because they're going to be on the stage with a guy who's saying, 'Hey, what about this,' 'What about that,' 'What are you talking about?' And to the extent that he does that, he has contributed to the body politic something that needs to be there."

But the reality of politics, McDermott said, is that electoral success means compromise, and being right in the past on something like a failed war that a majority of Americans initially backed doesn't necessarily make a good platform.

To illustrate this, McDermott told of taking his staff recently to see one of his favorite statues in the capitol. It's a likeness of Ernest Gruening, a Democratic senator from Alaska in the 1960s. McDermott's young staffers had no idea who Ernest Gruening was. Gruening, McDermott pointedly explained, was one of two senators to vote against the Gulf of Tonkin resolution authorizing the Vietnam war. Now he's a nobody.

Kucinich likes to remind everyone who will listen that he was right to vote against the Iraq War, that he is somebody because of that, should even be elected president because of that.

McDermott, who also voted against the Iraq War, sees it differently. "The guys who had the perspicacity to see it can't be upset by the fact that nobody gives them credit for it," he said.

Dennis Kucinich can and will be upset by this lack of credit. He seems ready to run a whole primary campaign around his need for recognition for being right on Iraq. He's run this kind of campaign in the past, to great success. But feelings about the Iraq War are not as settled in this country as feelings about the Muni Light affair are in Cleveland. A slogan like "Because he was right" might not even be enough for a political rock star like Barack Obama this season; given that, there's not much reason to think it will put Kucinich over the top.

Maybe some day Kucinich will get the credit he feels he deserves for being among the few who were right about the Iraq War all along. Maybe someone will build a statue of him somewhere. Perhaps it will even be intended as a monument to his rightness about a disastrous war. Perhaps, then, young people will be taken occasionally to view this statue, and perhaps some wise older person will occasionally tell young people who Kucinich was and, for a brief moment, before they forget that they ever heard his name, these future voters will give Kucinich what he so desperately craves: vindication.

But odds are better that Kucinich, like Ernest Gruening, will be a nobody one day too—and probably a lot sooner than he thinks.

The "Second Tier":
Dodd, Biden, Richardson, Gravel

JAMES RIDGEWAY

The Also-Rans

When it comes to winning their party's nomination, the chances of the Democratic candidates described in this chapter run from slim to none. This fact has little to do with their qualifications to be president, which generally match or exceed those of the three leaders. Instead, it has to do with their success as *candidates* for the presidency— which in turn, depends upon their performance in campaigning and fundraising.

Delaware senator Joe Biden, arguably the best qualified of the entire Democratic lineup, is a clumsy candidate with a talent for making stupid (or plagiarized) statements. As of June 30, 2007, he had raised only $4 million—not much more than 10 percent of Hillary Clinton's campaign chest. Former New Mexico governor Bill Richardson, who has executive, cabinet, and international experience, comes off as affable but clueless, and had $6 million. Connecticut senator Chris Dodd, a thirty-three year Congressional veteran, had managed to raise almost $9 million—still less than a fourth of Clinton's money and a third of Obama's— but is fatally stiff and nerdy (an uncool kind of nerdy, as opposed to the cool nerdiness of Mike Gravel).

In various polls, these candidates' likely share of primary votes runs from a rare high of 10 percent (for Richardson in early-primary states) to a low of less than 1 percent; in several polls, some or all of them trail Dennis Kucinich. But unlike reform or "protest" candidates Kucinich and Gravel, who are running to raise issues and take positions absent from the mainstream Democratic agenda, these three members of the second string fall well within the mainstream themselves, and do not differ categorically from the frontrunners. So why did they toss their hats in the ring to start with—and why do they remain in a race (as of this writing in July 2007) they cannot hope to win? Clearly, because they hope to get something out of it. That something is most likely a plum position in an Obama, Edwards, or especially a Hillary Clinton administration.

Richardson, who served in Bill Clinton's cabinet and could be a draw for Latino and Southwestern voters, has long been discussed as a possible vice president under Hillary, where he would be agreeably pleasant and unthreatening. The wonky and well-placed Dodd is ripe for any number of cabinet seats, from Treasury to State. And Biden, whose reputation as a foreign policy maven might outweigh his penchant for undiplomatic flubs, was rumored to be in line for secretary of state had John Kerry won. If he doesn't get that this time, he could serve as ambassador to the UN or as a special envoy to world trouble spots (those rejected by Bill Clinton, that is).

In return, each of these lesser candidates brings campaign capital to the table—beyond their few primary voters and even fewer (if any) convention delegates—that might make them valuable to any of the frontrunners.

CHRISTOPHER DODD

Christopher Dodd has sought to position himself as a "fresh face with experience," turning his relative anonymity into a virtue and suggesting that he represents some sort of alternative to the leading candidates. But the senior senator from Connecticut is in fact a consummate Democratic political insider. An ebullient Irish American politician somewhat in the mold of Ted Kennedy and Daniel Patrick Moynihan, he has become a powerful force in the Senate. Now in his fifth Senate term (following three terms in the House), Dodd has occupied important committee seats and is considered a formidable deal-maker. He chaired the Democratic National Committee during the heart of the Clinton years, from 1995 to 1997.

Reliably liberal on most issues—he has an 80 percent "composite liberal rating" from the *National Journal*, the same as Hillary Clinton's—Dodd is just as reliably corporate-friendly when it comes to the industries that matter most to him. The banking, investment, and insurance industries can count Dodd among their best friends on the left side of the aisle—and he, in turn, can count them among his leading campaign contributors. In the 2008 primary field, he stands out as the candidate of Wall Street.

Like George W. Bush, Dodd was born into a well-known Connecticut political family, though one of considerably more modest means. Dodd's father, Thomas J. Dodd, served two terms in the Senate between 1954 and 1970 (interrupted by a loss to W.'s grandfather, Prescott Bush). A former FBI agent and official in FDR's Justice Department, Thomas Dodd became famous as a lead prosecutor at the Nuremberg Trials. He was also a staunch anti-communist and a supporter of the Vietnam

War (and immortalized as such in Phil Ochs's "Draft Dodger Rag": "I believe in God and Senator Dodd and keeping old Castro down").

Christopher Dodd came of age in the 1960s, and served in both the Peace Corps and US Army Reserve before his election to Congress in 1974, at the age of thirty. One of the so-called Watergate Babies—young Democrats propelled into office following Nixon's resignation—Dodd represented Connecticut's fairly conservative (and often Republican) second district: not the Cheeveresque Connecticut of the popular imagination, but the fishermen, tobacco farmers, and military bases of the state's eastern end. In 1980, he moved on to the Senate, thus expanding his constituency to include the bankers and brokers of the wealthy New York suburbs, and the insurance industry long based around Hartford.

On foreign policy, Dodd has been known for his keen interest in Latin America, first developed during his Peace Corps years in the Dominican Republic. He has advocated a path of more accommodation with Cuba, opposed support for the military junta in El Salvador and the Contras in Nicaragua, and argued that Sandinistas were a legitimate democratic government. More recently he opposed Otto Reich's nomination as assistant secretary of state in 2002, claiming Reich was behind an abortive coup against Hugo Chavez; he met with Chavez in 2005 and called for an easing of tensions between the United States and Venezuela.

Dodd voted for the 2002 resolution authorizing Bush to launch the Iraq War. He has now been a critic of the war and of the weakness of the Democratic response, particularly to Bush's 2007 troop surge. He voted against

Iraq-Afghanistan supplemental funding in May 2007, as did Clinton, Obama, and of course Kucinich. Dodd also supports the more aggressive of the Congressional plans to end the war, which has split Democrats. In an April speech in Iowa, Dodd said, "I am calling on all the candidates in this race to join me in clearly standing up to the president once and for all by stating their support for the Feingold-Reid legislation that sets a firm timetable to end this war by March 3, 2008."

Dodd has a predictable progressive voting record on current environmental issues (he would limit carbon emissions by 80 percent by 2050, create a carbon tax, institute higher fuel efficiency standards, and support alternative fuels, and he opposes polluting coal-to-oil technologies); on reproductive rights (he opposed the ban on so-called partial birth abortions because it does not include an exception to protect a woman's health); and on civil liberties (he co-sponsored the "Restoring the Constitution Act of 2007," which restores Habeas Corpus rights, bars evidence gained through torture or coercion, and reinstates US adherence to the Geneva Conventions in order to protect the nation's military personnel abroad).[1] His healthcare plan has more specifics than some, but depends, like most of the candidates' plans, on expanding government support for health insurance coverage—in effect, corporate welfare for the insurance industry.

Dodd has taken liberal positions on the funding of the welfare state, as well, and he seeks to depict himself as a champion of ordinary low- and middle-income Americans. But Dodd is tightly bound to Wall Street. Connecticut long served as home to insurance companies, and like all politicians from that state, he pays them obeisance; the insurance industry, however, has begun to diversify out of Connecticut in recent years. Dodd, meanwhile, has grown closer to Wall Street financial interests, doing the grunt work on Capital Hill for legislation that reduces government oversight. He was an important player in the transformations of the 1990s, when banks and securities firms merged, and when the credit card became a principal means of debt financing in the United States.

Dodd was an original co-sponsor of 1995 legislation making it more difficult for people to sue corporations, allowing judges to decide which plaintiffs were worthy, and limiting judgments in cases where the companies could successfully claim they didn't know they were committing fraud. His defining moment came when Bill Clinton vetoed the bill. As the *Journal of Accountancy* noted, "Perhaps the bill's strongest supporter in Congress, Senator Christopher J. Dodd . . . urged both House and Senate Democrats to override Clinton's veto, even if it amounted to a defeat of the intent of his own party's president."

In 1998, the group Public Campaign gave Dodd a "Golden Leash Award," which it calls "a symbol of the ties between special interest money and elected officials. It is awarded to members of Congress who demonstrate egregious conduct in the quid pro quo practice of dollar democracy":

> This award serves as a reminder of Senator Dodd's acceptance of $910,304 in campaign cash from January 1993 to December 1997 from the Securities, Investment, Accounting and High-Tech Computer industries . . . Goldman, Sachs & Co., Morgan Stanley, Salomon Brothers and others

donat[ed] $523,551 in PAC and individual contributions. The accounting industry—perhaps the biggest winners in the 1995 securities litigation reform law—donated $345,903 in PAC and individual contributions. This includes such giants as Price Waterhouse, Ernst & Young, and Coopers & Lybrand, among others. Deloitte & Touche's contributions to Senator Dodd increased nearly five-fold from 1995 to 1996 soon after Congress passed the reform law the industry championed. The computer industry—a fairly new player in the campaign contribution field—ponied up $40,850 in contributions.[2]

Dodd's record is not entirely one-sided. He has taken positions against extreme predatory lending practices, for example, and he voted against the 2005 bankruptcy bill, which was considered a gift to the banks and other credit card lenders at the expense of consumers. But his close ties to the financial sector remain troubling, all the more so in view of his recent ascendancy to the chair of the powerful Senate Banking Committee, giving him oversight of the banking, financial services, and insurance industries. On the eve of the Democratic takeover of Congress (and of Dodd's announcement of his candidacy), Massie Ritsch of the government watchdog group the Center for Responsive Politics told the *Washington Post*, "It's a tightrope walk when you're the chairman of a committee that regulates the industry that gives the most money to politics, in general. . . . It has to be tempting to take a lot of money from this industry, because they want to give it so much."

Dodd, clearly, has long given in to temptation, and has

no intention of stopping now. The biggest funders of his presidential campaigns, as of his recent Senate campaigns, come from the finance sector. A February 2007 report from the Bloomberg News service, which is displayed on Dodd's own campaign website (whether out of pride or full disclosure is not clear), describes it best:

> Senator Christopher Dodd, trailing in presidential polls, ran ahead of his Democratic rivals in the race for money in the last quarter of 2006, propelled by contributions from the financial-services industry that he oversees.
>
> Donations from employees of American International Group Inc., Citigroup Inc. and Merrill Lynch & Co. Inc. helped Dodd, the new chairman of the Senate Banking Committee, raise $3 million over the final three months of last year, according to Federal Election Commission records. The Connecticut Democrat raised more than any other candidate, Democrat or Republican—even edging New York Senator Hillary Clinton.
>
> All told, employees of financial-services firms contributed more than $1 million of Dodd's total. The Senate banking panel "is a juice committee," said Craig Holman, a lobbyist for Public Citizen, a Washington group that supports tougher ethics laws. "The industry feels the pressure to give because this is the chairman with oversight over their business affairs." Dodd, 62, said in an interview that he has long-standing ties to members of the financial community. "This is not a newfound relationship," he said. "These people know me

best. They've worked with me. I've worked with them. We've been in agreement on various issues; we've been in disagreement on various issues over the years."

Also revealing is a profile in the *New York Observer* describing a fundraising event at an upscale New York venue:

> Dozens of men in business suits and women in expensive heels emptied out of black Lincoln Town Cars for the event, which raised about a half-million dollars for Mr. Dodd's political-action committee. Mitch Krieger, a 38-year-old money manager in a pinstriped shirt, attended the fundraiser as a favor to a friend and client. Like many other donors who paid at least $1,000 to meet the senator, Mr. Krieger said he wanted to get to know Mr. Dodd better.

The profile—which described Dodd as "affable," "amicable," and "convivial"—also mentioned the presence of minor Hollywood stars (as well as legendary financier Felix Rohatyn), and noted that before his second marriage, Dodd was considered "one of Washington's most eligible bachelors. He danced nearly into the small hours with a woman in a Budapest hotel and dated Bianca Jagger and Carrie Fisher." This seems consistent with the image Dodd himself is seeking to cast: while he rakes in money from button-down types and gives stodgy debate performances, Dodd nonetheless positions himself as a fun, hip guy—a stud, even, with his younger wife and toddler daughter. "I am the only candidate who receives mailing from both AARP and diaper services," the sixty-three-year-old senator told crowds in Iowa in July. He first announced his candidacy, unfortuitously, on the Don Imus show; has campaigned with his old friend musician Paul Simon; and shares his personal iPod playlists at a web page called DoddPod.

JOSEPH R. BIDEN, JR.

Like Dodd, Delaware's longtime senator Joseph R. Biden, Jr., is generally quite liberal in his opinions and voting record—he received the same 80 percent "composite liberal" rating from the *National Journal*—but nonetheless tries to position himself as running in the middle. What sets him apart from the other candidates, more than anything, is his take on Iraq—and more generally, on the role of the United States in a post-Cold War world. Repeatedly, over the past two decades, Biden has advocated for strong US intervention in trouble spots around the world (including the one created by the Bush administration in Iraq) in the name of democracy and human rights, a well-intentioned but highly risky stance that has won him devoted support as well as widespread opposition.

Biden—again, like Dodd—has spent the better part of his adult life in the United States Congress. The son of a car salesman from suburban Wilmington, Biden was twenty-nine years old when he ran for the Senate in 1972. His only political experience was two years in the New Castle County Council. His surprise victory, against longtime senator and former governor Caleb Boggs, launched what would be the first of six Senate terms.

Biden became a nationally recognized face while chairing the Senate Judiciary Committee from 1987 to 1995, when presiding over televised hearings on controversial Supreme Court nominations of Robert Bork—a lone triumphant moment for liberal Democrats—and Clarence Thomas. Many women's groups complained about what they felt was Biden's harsh treatment of Anita Hill, and many progressives have never forgiven him for his vote to confirm Thomas.

Biden is also credited for authoring several significant pieces of legislation in the area of federal law enforcement. The Violent Crime Control and Law Enforcement Act of 1994, widely known as the Biden law, banned the manufacture of nineteen specific semiautomatic "assault weapons." It also allocated more money to build prisons and sets up bootcamps for delinquent minors. It designated fifty new federal offenses, including gang membership, and created several new federal death penalty offenses, including murders related to drug dealing, drive-by shooting murders, civil rights-related murders, murders of federal law enforcement officers, and death caused by acts of terrorism or weapons of mass destruction. (The law was passed shortly before the Oklahoma City bombing, and its provisions were applied to execute Timothy McVeigh.) The legislation received bipartisan support, but was reviled by death penalty opponents and civil libertarians. Some believe it broke ground for the Antiterrorism and Effective Death Penalty Act of 1996, the sweeping post-Oklahoma City legislation signed into law by Bill Clinton, which in turn paved the way for the USA PATRIOT Act of 2001.

One section of the Biden law was the Violence Against Women Act (VAWA), which provided new measures and increased federal funding to combat domestic violence, rape, and other gender-based crimes. (A portion of VAWA was ruled unconstitutional by the Supreme Court in 2000, but the rest was reauthorized in 2000 and again in 2005.) Biden is generally considered a strong supporter of women's rights, although he supported the ban on late-term abortions and he has opposed federal funding for abortions.

On other domestic issues, Biden has sought to take the lead on drug policy, spearheading creation of a "Drug Czar" and crafting laws to control narcotics—measures that are widely viewed as pretty much of a failure. He supports the Bush immigration plan, with both its "amnesty" for existing undocumented residents and its big border fence to keep new ones out. His plan for dealing with the healthcare crisis is vague to nonexistent, with references to containing costs by "modernizing" and "simplifying" the system; "expanding" health insurance; and looking at "innovative alternatives" pioneered by the states to "evaluate what works best in providing affordable access to healthcare for all." On climate change he occupies what has become the conventional liberal middleground, supporting a "'cap and trade' approach to regulating emissions and investment in technologies" to reduce greenhouse gasses. Like all of the mainstream candidates, he is beholden to corporate interests who support his campaigns or dominate his state; in Biden's case, he cast a noteworthy vote in favor of the controversial 2005 bankruptcy bill, which was a boon to credit card lenders, many of which are based in Delaware due to lax state regulations. Biden's biggest single block of support is trial lawyers, who like his strong position against tort reform.

It is in foreign policy, most of all, where Biden has sought to make his mark, and he has had a bully pulpit on the Senate Foreign Relations Committee, where he has been chair or ranking minority member since the late 1990s. In recent decades, he has consistently taken an interventionist stance, promoting the idea that the United States, as the lone remaining superpower, ought to step in—with the UN, with NATO, or on its own—to prevent genocide, keep the peace, and promote democracy. Under Clinton, he pushed for intervention in Bosnia, and supported NATO's intervention in Kosovo. More recently, he has argued for an immediate intercession in Darfur, with US troops if need be.

Biden, like all of the candidates then in Congress save Dennis Kucinich, voted in favor of the 2002 Iraq War Resolution. He became an early and consistent critic. During a 2005 interview with Salon.com, Biden recanted his vote, saying, "I never figured on the absolute incompetence of the administration. . . . If I knew Cheney and Rumsfeld so wholly possessed the president's attention, I never would have voted for that." (It is unclear what Biden thinks would have happened if the president had kept his own counsel; on campaign stops he now describes Bush as "brain dead.")

Biden favors a phased troop withdrawal down to a "residual" force, but made enemies by voting for the May 2007 supplemental war funding bill, insisting that a no-vote would constitute abandoning the troops. But he also favors a controversial plan that differs from any of the other candidates—as he describes it, a "third way":

> President Bush does not have a strategy for victory in Iraq. His strategy is to prevent defeat and to hand the problem off to his successor. As a result, more and more Americans understandably want a

rapid withdrawal, even at the risk of trading a dictator for chaos and a civil war that could become a regional war. Both are bad alternatives.

There is a third way that can achieve the two objectives most Americans share: to bring our troops home without leaving chaos behind. The idea is to maintain a unified Iraq by federalizing it and giving Kurds, Shiites and Sunnis breathing room in their own regions.[3]

Biden insists that we have to destroy the country in order to save it. He says the only way to solve the bloody mess the Unites States has created is through what amounts to a partition, providing autonomous states for the main ethnic and religious groups, with the whole thing monitored by a UN-sponsored Iraq Oversight Group. Under a plan crafted along with Leslie Gelb, former chair of the Council on Foreign Relations, a central government would sit atop of this regional setup, responsible for "common interests, like border security and the distribution of oil revenues." The latter is meant to assuage the Sunnis, who would have no oil their region, unlike the Kurds, who control the big northern oilfields around Kirkuk, and the Shia, with even larger reserves in the south. In reality, these oil resources would most likely be offered for lease to foreign companies under production sharing agreements, restoring Iraq to an earlier status: The country, after all, was once a colonial appendage of Britain before World War I, acquired solely for its oil. Biden alluded to the parallel himself in a February 2007 interview with Maureen Dowd: "Any country that comes into being as a consequence of the pen of a diplomat has never been able to be stable except by (a) an imperial power dominating it, (b) a dictator or strongman, or (c) a federal system." Biden clearly believes in the third of these options, but in practice his plan may well recreate the first.

Biden ran for president twenty years ago, seeking the 1988 Democratic nomination. His campaign blew up when he repeated nearly verbatim a speech by Neil Kinnock, then leader of the British Labour Party. He had credited Kinnock in previous instances when he used the speech, but failed to do so in one case, which was caught on video (and distributed to the press, along with a video of Kinnock, by aides to Michael Dukakis). He quit the campaign in September of 1987.

The rhetorical adroitness of Kinnock's speech should in itself have tipped off anyone to the fact that it wasn't Biden's. The senator is known as a speaker who never uses one word when he can use three. Describing the confirmation hearings of Supreme Court nominee Samuel Alito, the *Washington Post*'s Dana Millbank wrote:

> Sen. Joseph R. Biden Jr. (D-Del.), in his first 12 minutes of questioning the nominee, managed to get off only one question. Instead, during his 30-minute round of questioning, Biden spoke about his own Irish American roots, his "Grandfather Finnegan," his son's application to Princeton (he attended the University of Pennsylvania instead, Biden said), a speech the senator gave on the Princeton campus, the fact that Biden is "not a Princeton fan," and his views on the eyeglasses of Sen. Dianne Feinstein (D-Calif.).

Biden has also made several campaign-killing statements since he declared his candidacy in January 2007. Within days, he said, in an apparent effort to compliment rival Barak Obama, "I mean, you got the first mainstream African-American who is articulate and bright and clean and a nice-looking guy . . . I mean, that's a storybook, man." After Biden apologized, Jesse Jackson defended him, saying "To me, this was a gaffe, not a statement about his philosophy or ideology."

Indeed, there is no evidence that Biden is any more racist than any other middle-aged white American. Yet six months after the Obama fiasco, he declared, in an apparent effort to compliment Americans of Indian descent, "In Delaware, the largest growth in population is Indian Americans—moving from India. You cannot go to a 7-11 or a Dunkin' Donuts unless you have a slight Indian accent. I'm not joking." His office sought to explain the remarks, saying, "The point Senator Biden was making is that there has been a vibrant Indian-American community in Delaware for decades. It has primarily been made up of engineers, scientists and physicians, but more recently, middle-class families are moving into Delaware and purchasing family-run small businesses."

Nevertheless, it is quite possible that, as *Washington Post* columnist Richard Cohen put it, "Biden's manic-obsessive running of the mouth has become the functional equivalent of womanizing or some other character weakness that disqualifies a man for the presidency."

BILL RICHARDSON

New Mexico governor Bill Richardson has been floated many times as a potential vice presidential candidate—for

Bill Richardson

Al Gore in 2000, John Kerry in 2004, and now for Hillary Clinton—and it isn't difficult to see why. On paper, Richardson brings to the table many things that could be assets to any Democratic presidential campaign. He brings experience ranging from executive (as New Mexico governor, where he is now in his second term); to cabinet (as Bill Clinton's secretary of energy); to international (as UN Ambassador under Clinton); to congressional (representing northern New Mexico in the House from 1982 to 1997). It's a resume that belies his public performance as a candidate, where he often seems surprisingly inarticulate, inconsistent, and inept. (One has to believe he must be better than this behind closed doors, since he's been nominated for the Nobel Peace Prize based on his negotiation skills.)

As a Southwestern Hispanic (the term he prefers), Richardson also embodies geographic and cultural diversity, and could draw contested states and ethnic constituencies to the Democrats. His record could attract other swing voters as well. He is well-liked by the NRA, which backed him in his races for governor, and by the libertarian Cato Institute, which gave him the highest score of any Democratic governor on its "Fiscal Policy Report Card" for "cutting taxes and strictly limiting increases in state spending."[4]

In most of his current issue statements, including his fuzzy healthcare plan, he stresses that he can do the job without raising taxes. Libertarian political consultant Liz Mair, writing in the *New York Sun* in March, pointed to Richardson's broad appeal and noted that "Kerry only would have needed 70,000 voters in New Mexico, Colorado, and Nevada (folks who, presumably, want to keep both their money and their guns) to flip the electoral college in 2004."

Richardson's reputation for being corporate-friendly might win him some moderate support as well. But his history of close ties to the oil and gas corporations includes seriously compromising—and generally underreported—conflicts of interest, and should dissuade any voter who believes the White House has been in the pocket of the petroleum industry for long enough.

While William Blaine Richardson III is of three-quarters Mexican descent, it's the other quarter that gave him his name, and he had a tonier upbringing than any of the other Democratic candidates: a well-off childhood in Mexico City as son of a Citibank executive, and prep school in Massachusetts. None of this reduces his significance as the first Latino presidential candidate, at a time when Latinos, by far the fastest-growing portion of the population, are becoming a force in national elections—and could become much more so if inspired to register and vote in larger numbers. These are votes the Democrats can by no means count on: In 2004, Bush won 42 percent of the more than 7 million Latino votes, and first-time Latino voters were split almost evenly between Bush and Kerry. Bush also won the Latino vote in Florida in both 2004 and 2000.

Because of his Mexican roots and his governorship of a border state, Richardson is in a position to play a particularly important role in the politics of immigration, which has emerged, along with healthcare, as the most burning political issue of the day. In 2007, he first supported Bush's compromise plan, which calls for a fence on the Mexican border and a controversial guest worker pro-

Bill Richardson

gram, as well as a plan that allows illegal immigrants living here to buy their way to citizenship. Then he reversed himself and took a stand against the fence. In general, he argued that whatever happens on the border should be aimed at keeping families together and not breaking them apart. "I believe we have to bring the 12 million undocumented workers out of the shadows, set up a standard where they speak English, if they pass background checks, pay back taxes, obey the laws, embrace American values, give them a chance, a path to citizenship, not amnesty." But he also seeks to show that he is tough on illegal immigration, highlighting "securing the border" as the first point in his immigration plan and pushing for increased enforcement on the Mexican as well as the US side. In 2005, Richardson declared a state of emergency in New Mexico's four border counties, which released $1.75 million in state funds for overtime pay to local police forces to fight illegal immigration.

Richardson positions himself strongly as a man of the West—the Southwest and Mountain West, rather than the West Coast—down to his cowboy boots and string tie. As part of this image, he promotes his support of gun ownership, which dates back to his opposition in Congress to the 1993 Brady Bill. When the National Rifle Association endorsed him in his second run for governor in 2006, Richardson joined them for the announcement at the NRA-sponsored National Police Shooting Championships, held, according to the group's website, at "a new, state-of-the-art facility in Albuquerque's Shooting Range Park, made possible with $1.4 million in funding and vigorous support from New Mexico governor Bill Richardson and Mayor Martin Chavez." The NRA's executive director reported that Richardson "has treated us first class." Richardson, who supported a law allowing New Mexicans to carry concealed weapons, told an appreciative crowd that he had a concealed-carry permit himself. "I am not packing today, though, because I have plenty of State Police officers here to protect me."

Richardson has sought to depict himself as among the most fervent antiwar candidates. From his position outside of Congress, he has urged Congress members to use what he says is their power to reverse their 2002 authorization for the Iraq War. "Congress has a public mandate and the Constitutional authority to end this war. If you de-authorize, we could have our ALL troops home in six months."

Richardson has also promoted himself as a leading "clean energy" advocate, in the cabinet, the New Mexico statehouse, and in his current campaign. His website urges voters to "Join Bill's Call for a New Energy Revolution":

> In order to make America a Clean Energy Nation, as I made New Mexico a Clean Energy State, we need a man-on-the-moon program to end our addiction to oil and abate our global warming crisis. And we need to do it much faster and much more boldly than most people are suggesting. Some politicians and some industry people will say we can't do what I propose—I say we need to change fast or sink slowly. Now is the time for bold actions, clear vision, and complete commitment.
>
> Consider this a call to action, for Congress, the energy industry, and the public. I am calling for a New American Revolution—an energy and climate revolution. And I am calling on you to join it.

The trail of money—and facts—tells a different story. As befits a leading politician from one of the nation's historic bastions of oil and gas, Richardson has a network of connections with the petroleum industry. As of July 2003, of all the candidates—in both parties—he ranked fifth as recipient of oil and gas money. Top energy contributors include the oil services company Lucky Services, WWC Engineering, Western Refining, and Xcel Energy. He sat on the boards of directors of three large oil companies—San Antonio-based Valero Energy Corp, Houston-based Diamond Offshore Drilling, and Denver-based Venoco. All three of these companies are engaged in controversial business operations that can often put them at loggerheads with environmentalists. Richardson's resignation from the boards accompanied his announcement of a clean energy initiative in his first campaign for governor. He would later call New Mexico the most environmentally progressive state in the union.

Valero, the nation's largest independent refinery, paid Richardson (as a non-employee director) $25,000 a year in 2001 until June 2002. He also owned stock in Valero worth between $100,001 and $250,000, and had stock options valued between $250,001 and $500,000, according to disclosures filed with the Federal Election Commission. He exercised his options and sold all of his stock only in May 2007, saying it had become a "distraction" in his campaign and "because I was getting questions, I just felt it was best to divest myself." Of course, one of the principal energy issues of the day is whether or not to build more refineries in the United States; the industry claims it is being blocked by environmentalists.

Diamond Drilling, the offshore exploration firm with

deep Republican ties on whose board Richardson served in 2001 and 2002, is engaged in offshore drilling platforms and is an amalgam of three earlier companies, including Zapata Oil. Zapata pioneered the offshore rig and was formed by George Herbert Walker Bush along with Tom Devine—a former CIA officer who, according to classified documents released this year, continued to work for the agency while in his new role at Zapata—and the Liedke brothers, who had close ties to the Bush family and went on to found the big Pennzoil pipeline business.

Venoco, the third company that once had Richardson on its board, is an oil producer with a first-of-its-kind controversial drilling project in a state sanctuary off the coast near Santa Barbara, where it wants to get at the oil reserve by drilling horizontally out from the shore. In addition to more oil, the wells could yield substantial amounts of natural gas.

Among Richardson's most prominent current campaign backers is Xcel Corporation, the old Northern States Power Company, an electric utility behemoth with tentacles stretching across the upper Midwest and mountain states. Its power is coal-fired, and among its projects is a spanking new "alternative energy" scheme to turn coal into gas, an expensive and environmentally ruinous approach to energy production. Coal gassification projects would strip-mine the Fort Union formation, one of the nation's largest seams of coal running across the eastern front of the Rockies.

Then there was the Peregrine Systems scandal, a financial scam in the Enron style. Peregrine was a San Diego-based software company controlled by John Moores, a real estate operator, owner of the Padres, and a

Richardson (and Clinton) supporter. The CEO was Stephen Gardner, brother-in-law of Richardson's wife. Richardson was put on the board, where he sat as an outside director from February 2001 to June 2002. During this period of time, the directors were trying to hide financial dealings, including non-existent sales, and hiding the severity of its losses with phony accounting that included pumping up revenues by 40 percent. The company eventually went into bankruptcy and Gardner was later charged with obstruction of justice and securities fraud. When he ran for governor in New Mexico, Richardson got away with claiming "I had no involvement because I was what was called an 'outside director'"—he didn't attend numerous meetings and "didn't have time" to read corporate reports, he said (though at the same time, he insisted he had discharged his corporate duties). But according to Don Bauder in the *San Diego Reader*, "Records show that Richardson attended, in person or by phone, 15 board meetings. In those meetings, directors were hearing that the company might get caught cooking the books." With regard to one shady deal, "The directors were told that the Securities and Exchange Commission had questioned three Peregrine top executives and a national business magazine was on the story. Directors discussed how to spin it." In May of 2002, when the company announced it had found accounting irregularities, the stock collapsed, and regulators began investigating. Richardson resigned in June. Before that, he had issued some eyebrow-arching statements. After the horse was out of the barn, he sent a letter to the board saying there should be an accounting investigation. Then he told New Mexico voters that he had helped to uncover the cooked books because he had voted to replace the accounting firm of Arthur Andersen with a new firm, KPMG. But KPMG got booted after two months, and it was then that the fraud came out.

Least palatable of all would be Richardson's stint, during that same period of 2001 to 2002 as senior managing director of Kissinger McLarty Associates, an international strategic advisory firm specializing in Latin America and international energy issues. The firm was formed by the merger of two organizations headed by former Secretary of State Henry Kissinger and Mack McLarty, who served as President Clinton's chief of staff. No mention is made of the association on Richardson's campaign website.

For others, the low point of Richardson's career might involve the railroading of Wen Ho Lee, the scientist who worked at Los Alamos nuclear lab, which was under the control of Richardson's Department of Energy. In 1999, the scientist was accused of stealing documents containing the design of a modern US nuclear warhead and giving it to China. Lee was fired after the FBI began investigating him, and that same day, his name was leaked to the press. There was wide speculation that Richardson himself had leaked the information about Lee, although reporters would not divulge their source. (In 2006, the US government and five media outlets, including the *New York Times* and the *Washington Post*, jointly paid Lee a total of $1.6 million to settle allegations that government leaks violated his privacy.) Lee was arrested and held for almost a year in solitary confinement. The charges turned out to be specious—Lee had never had access to the documents in question—but Lee pled guilty in a plea bargain to a felony count of improperly downloading restricted data, for moving classified files onto an unauthorized computer. Richardson still says, "I stand behind the very strong actions that I took to protect our nuclear secrets."

The Gadfly

From the moment he bulldozed his way into public consciousness, maverick candidate Mike Gravel has been a pain in the ass of the Democratic establishment—exactly what he wants to be.

For a year, the party mainstream had simply ignored the seventy-six-year-old former senator from Alaska, who declared his candidacy months before any of the other Democratic contenders, back in April 2006. Such a small and insignificant gadfly, it seemed, wasn't even worth the effort of swatting. That attitude ended with Gravel's appearance at a sleepy Democratic presidential debate in South Carolina. After challenging his rivals to end the war by legislative fiat—and make it a felony for the president to keep troops in Iraq—Gravel saw visits to his website zoom up, and YouTube clips of his debate remarks and even his campaign videos began drawing tens of thousands of views.

Gravel is less polite than Dennis Kucinich, whom he joins in challenging the other candidates on their timid and pathologically centrist positions. One-on-one, Mike Gravel is jovial and mild-mannered; on stage with his rivals, he's mad as hell, and he's not going to take it any more, shaking things up with a dreck-cutting matter-of-factness. Commenting that his fellow candidates frightened him because they refused to take the nuclear option off the table with regard to Iran, he then confronted Obama with the question, "Tell me, Barack, who do you want to nuke?" Addressing his old Senate colleague Joe Biden on his plans for Iraq's future, he spoke of the arrogance of wanting to direct the government of another country—to which Biden replied that Gravel was living in "happy land."

In fact, it could be argued that Gravel's so-called tirades, especially on the Iraq War, result not from naivete, but from a kind of experience that none of the other candidates share. Until the debate, Gravel's low-budget campaign may have been nearly invisible. Yet to older progressives, Gravel is hardly an unknown. During the 1960s, he was often in the news as one of Congress's fiercest opponents of the Vietnam War. In his most famous act, Gravel helped make public the Pentagon Papers by carrying them into the Senate in two suitcases and reading them into the record—for a time, with tears streaming down his face. In a television interview he said, "I wept because it hurts . . . to see our nation dragged in the mud . . . to be part of a nation that is killing innocent human beings."[5] Gravel is also credited with mounting filibusters and cutting legislative deals that helped stop the draft, and later with fighting nuclear testing and nuclear power.

Born into a working-class French Canadian family in central Massachusetts and educated in Catholic schools, Gravel moved to Alaska after serving a stint in the Army Counter Intelligence Corps in the 1950s. He worked as a brakeman on the Alaska Railroad and made some money as a property developer on the Kenai Peninsula before winning a seat in the state legislature and then the US Senate. He lost that seat in 1980, in the election that would send Republican Frank Murkowski to Washington. After twelve years in Congress, Gravel told Salon.com he had alienated "almost every constituency in Alaska," and he was disgusted "with public service, with the way government operated."

Returning to Alaska from Washington, Gravel worked as a real estate developer, stockbroker, and consultant. One of his real estate deals went belly up and into bankruptcy. Then, in 1989 Gravel, back in Arlington, Virginia, re-emerged as head of something called the Democracy Foundation. Here he promoted a form of direct democracy, with a plan to pass an amendment to the Constitution that would make it possible for ordinary citizenry to directly propose and enact laws through an initiative process.

His "National Initiative for Democracy" forms the core of Gravel's politics. He advertises it with such slogans as "Let the People Decide" and "A Populist Concept of Democracy" (not completely accurate, but closer to the spirit of historical Populism than the pale imitation channeled by the rest of the Democratic field). In his summary of the initiative, Gravel declares, in language to set many a progressive heart beating: "The central power of government in a democracy is lawmaking—not voting. . . . Governments throughout history have been tools of oppression; they need not be." He then, however, adds this caveat: "American citizens can gain control of their government by becoming lawmakers and turning its purpose to public benefit, and stemming government growth—the people are more conservative than their elected officials regardless of political party." It's this kind of rhetoric that is winning Gravel fans among libertarians, who have helped make him an unlikely favorite on user-generated news sites like Digg.com (where some are hailing a ticket of "Mike Gravel/Ron Paul"—or vice versa).

The idea of direct democracy might have broad appeal to an electorate sick of a political system mired in soft money, corporate cronyism, and partisan gridlock. Nearly half the states already have procedures for initiative, referendum, and recall, and in places like California, citizens are fiercely attached to what sometimes amounts to their ballot box veto power. In one sense, then, Gravel is just trying to spread this already popular concept to the federal level.

But the system he proposes to create as a result of the Constitutional amendment suggests its own bureaucratic quagmire. For example, Gravel would have people propose a law through petition, or have it brought forward by a state legislature. However, he also added the idea of considering laws backed by a public opinion poll. This is a startling idea, since it is well known that opinion polls can easily be manipulated by the people who pay for them— through how questions are asked and where the sample is taken, and through the sleazy practices of push-polling.

Gravel insists the initiative process is "not intended to replace existing government, but to supplement it." Gravel's National Initiative would be carried out by an Electoral Trust, with one member elected at large from each state and a director appointed by the board of trustees. This Electoral Trust in effect creates a new political bureaucracy of people who can craft laws, operate a communications system, set up committees and run hearings. Like the Federal Reserve System, it lies outside the federal government structure, and is not appointed by or beholden to the president. It does its own accounting, though there also is accounting by the GAO. Money to run the system is to come from the federal Treasury.

When it comes to filling that Treasury, Gravel has another controversial proposal: to eliminate the income tax and fund the government solely through sales taxes. While appealing, again, to libertarians, the proposal is bound to alienate liberals who might otherwise sympathize with the ex-senator: Sales taxes are considered "regressive," meaning they take proportionately more from those with lower incomes than from the better-off. But Gravel maintains that since the present tax system has become corrupted by "wealthy people gaming the system," his fix would provide a solution; to help the poor, he'd provide a guaranteed minimum income, distributed through Social Security. Getting rid of the income tax was until fairly recently a topic relegated to the far right wing; but under Reagan and then Bush, Republicans began to talk about shelving the income tax and replacing it with a sales tax or a flat tax. It has been favored by such divergent figures as former presidential candidates Jerry Brown (in a liberal version that exempts a moderate portion of income) and Steve Forbes (in the conservative form, which taxes only wages and exempts capital gains).

On certain facets of social policy, Gravel happily goes out on a limb that the mainstream candidates, whatever their personal views, would never dare to test. He supports single-payer health system as a no-brainer. He insists, somewhat optimistically, that the American people would back gay marriage, if given the chance in a national initiative vote. Ditto on the war on drugs: "I think the American people realize the war on drugs is a total failure—waste of time, waste of money. What's wrong with marijuana? You can go out a buy a fifth of gin and do more damage to yourself."

Such proposals might be familiar fringe-candidate fare, but it is on the issue of the Iraq War that Gravel could prove embarrassing to the Democratic mainstream by relentlessly pointing out that Democrats could stop the war—if they choose to exercise their legislative power. "What we need to do is to create a constitutional confrontation between the Congress and the president," he says. "Most people have forgotten the Congress is more powerful than the president." Never mind impeachment, Gravel says: "That's a red herring right now. It would take over a year to screw around with it." Instead, he proposes a law commanding the president to bring the troops home. In sixty days. "The Democrats have the votes in the House to pass it. In the Senate, they will filibuster it. Fine. The Majority Leader starts a cloture vote the first day. Fails to get cloture. Fine. The next day—another vote on cloture. And the next day, and the next day, Saturdays and Sundays, no vacation—vote every single day. The dynamic is that now you give people enough time to weigh in and put pressure on those voting against cloture." (Here, Gravel knows whereof he speaks: As a senator, he filibustered legislation to extend the draft; eventually, a deal was cut to end it in two years.)

So, he goes on, "I would guess in fifteen to twenty days you would have cloture and the bill would pass and go to the president. He would veto it. Wonderful. It comes back to the House and Senate. Normal thing is to try to override and fail. No guts. No leadership. So in the House and Senate every day at noon, you have a vote to override the veto. The Democrats are the leaders—they control the calendar. It only takes half an hour to have these votes. The media will jump on it, you know, 'This guy changed his vote,' etc. But then peace groups can go out into the hustings and get these guys where they live, at home, and I would say that in thirty to forty-five days they will override the veto. But it's got to be on a clean, simple issue, none of this 'go out and manage the war, deal with the funds' stuff. We never cut off the funds in Vietnam. I was there. I tried it. I failed. What you have to do is go to their immediate survival. By Labor Day this could be all solved, and the troops be home by Christmas."

Thousands of Americans who may have no intention to vote for Gravel seem nontheless delighted to hear such no-nonsense challenges to mainsteam Democratic shuffling around the issue of the war. They also, apparently, are entertained not only by his debate antics, but by his campaign ads, which became a sensation on YouTube. In one, Gravel walks through the woods gathering kindling, then lights a campfire—which burns in closeup for seven more minutes while a foghorn sounds ominously in the background. In the real show-stopper, Gravel stares straight into the camera, his gaze steady, then finally he turns around and walks away along a shoreline. He pauses, stoops to pick up a rock, throws it in the water, and continues to walk into the distance. He speaks not a word in either ad.

These are not actually ads, Gravel explains, but the brainchild of "a couple of kids—a couple of young teachers—who drove up from Southern California" to make the videos, which show what Gravel's campaign "means to them." Gravel press secretary Alex Colwin explained the symbolism on NBC: "It would be the rock in the water and the ripple effect of the senator and his message and who he is, a man with an idea, who is little by little, day by day communicating that message." Gravel himself was characteristically blunt in response to ridiculing of the spots on Tucker Carlson's show: "It's a metaphor," he said. "Why can't people like you understand that?"

What does Gravel himself want his campaign to mean? Clearly, he hopes to push the leading Democratic candidates to the wall, at least on the question of Iraq. "There's one thing about politicians," he said. "They are like every other human being. They are interested in their own personal survival. And that's what's at stake—a dynamic that will ruin their political careers if they don't shape up."

Gravel, on the other hand, has no need to worry about his political career—and seems unconcerned about his "personal survival" in any but the most literal sense. In 2004, Gravel had run up $85,000 in credit card debt due to a health crisis requiring multiple surgeries, and the money he'd spent pursuing his National Initiative. Urged to declare personal bankruptcy, Gravel told Salon.com's Alex Koppelman, he at first hesitated. "And then I thought about it: 'My God, isn't this interesting? I'm going to get these six credit card companies who have been predators on normal people. I'm going to get them to contribute to the National Initiative.' And I filed bankruptcy just in a heartbeat, and that was it."

Through June 30, Gravel had spent just over $200,000 on his campaign—a hundred times less spending than leader Barack Obama, who stood at $22 million. While other candidates have their campaign buses, Gravel buys a ticket on Greyhound and sleeps on couches or at the local Motel 6. His only national visibility has come via the Internet and his presence at debates and forums, where he has succeeded in spooking the frontrunners.

At a July 12 NAACP forum, Gravel was in fine fettle, declaring, "I'm surprised it's so easy to get an applause from this group—all you have to do is dump on the Republican administration. This is a debate between Democrats. Where's the difference? Where do you think NAFTA came from? The trinity? It came from a Democratic administration." Later he advised the audience to "follow the money": "These others here, they're getting money from big pharma, they're getting money from the healthcare industry. MILLIONS! MILLIONS! You think they're free after they get to be president, that they're going to do something for you on healthcare?" Such tirades, no doubt, helped inspire John Edwards's post-forum whisper in Hillary Clinton's ear, caught by the microphone, that they "should try to have a more serious and a smaller group." The gadfly had become annoying enough to require crushing.

Add to this the fact that the Democratic leadership is haunted by the specter of Ralph Nader. While Dennis Kucinich—all in all a more reliable and effective advocate for left-leaning positions—can be counted on to drop out after the primaries and support the Democrat, Gravel is a true wild card. What would happen if old man Gravel bolted to run as an independent in the general election, and started pulling one or two or three points? (Keep in mind that nobody paid any heed to Nader in 2000 until he started running the dread campaign rallies in city after city, culminating in a screaming frenzy at Madison Square Garden.) To make matters worse, Nader himself has praised Gravel. After hearing Gravel speak before the Democratic National Committee, Nader called him "a fresh wind coming down from Alaska," complimented his National Initiative, and compared him to the Roman statesman and orator Cicero, who "defined freedom with these enduring words: 'Freedom is participation in power.'"

Commenting on the same speech, *Washington Post* columnist David Broder, the consummate Beltway insider, described the "disaster" of "the long harangue of former Alaska senator Mike Gravel, a strident critic of almost everything and promoter of a folly—a national initiative process—that not even a deranged blogger could love. Someone has to give him the hook before the real debates begin."

They only wish they could.

NOTES

1. See http://dodd.senate.gov/index.php?q=node/3741.
2. See http://www.sourcewatch.org/index.php?title=Christopher_John_Dodd.
3. See http://biden.senate.gov/newsroom/details.cfm?id=264509.
4. See http://www.cato.org/new/03-05/03-01-05r.html.
5. See http://www.beacon.org/client/client_pages/images/pentagon_35.pdf.

About the Contributors

LAURA FLANDERS, the host of *RadioNation* on Air America Radio, is the author of *Blue Grit: Democrats Take Back Politics from the Politicians* and *Bushwomen: How They Won the White House for Their Man.*

RICHARD GOLDSTEIN, a veteran commentator on culture, politics, and sexuality, is the author of *Homocons: The Rise of the Gay Right.*

DEAN KUIPERS, an editor at the *Los Angeles Times*, is the author of *Burning Rainbow Farm: How a Stoner Utopia Went Up in Smoke.*

JAMES RIDGEWAY is *Mother Jones*'s Washington, DC, bureau chief and author of *The Five Unanswered Questions about 9/11.*

ELI SANDERS is the senior staff writer for *The Stranger*, Seattle's weekly newspaper.

DAN SAVAGE is the author of the internationally syndicated sex column "Savage Love" and the editor of *The Stranger.*

AMY SCHOLDER is the editor in chief of Seven Stories Press.